TABLE OF CONTENTS:

FACE IT:

Reality, Freedom and the Computer Network
99 Theses for the Age of IT

Sand Sheff

Upheaval Dome Publishing

INTRODUCTION

I've got a story for you. It could well be the last thing you want to hear. Then again, it might be one of the last stories that really needs to be told.

It's about two worlds, two realities.

Which do you love more?

Stop for a second. Look up and look around. Maybe you're in your house or at the coffee shop or the airport or the park. You're in a place we used to call the real world; a place where we look at real faces, listen to real voices, feel the touch of true love.

Now, find a screen. That shouldn't be hard. Suddenly they're everywhere. Ok, are you ready? Bow your head to the screen. That's right, bow to the screen with your hands before you, maybe with a prayer of thanksgiving on your lips.

Don't want to do it? Me either. Then why do we do it all day long? Our heads bowed to screens, hands before us in the position of prayer, of submission. When you face the children with their faces to the screens, bowing their heads, does it look right? Does it bode well? Do you think our ancestors would be proud?

Now turn away from the machines and breathe in what surrounds us, the nature that's been given to us. There's a difference between nature and the machine. Life, consciousness and spirit live in the real moment. Nothing lives inside the screen.

We've been lured into a movie theater, and something is locking the doors behind us. What we leave behind is a place we once called reality. The theater doors are shutting. What will the feature film turn out to be?

We don't have to watch. Just like we don't have to hand our

preschoolers portable screens so they can be conditioned like little zombies for a world ruled and policed by machines. I don't care how cool and hip the relentless advertising campaigns are for these gadgets. I won't join in the chorus that heralds the dream of their new world, their alternate universe, where we turn our backs on nature and reality. Frankly, it makes me a little ill to see the glow of screens reflected on people's faces, especially mine. The Brave New Machine says:

"Hey, relax. It's just a show. Nowadays, everybody gets their own channel."

I'd rather be free.

One day we woke up and found ourselves surrounded by machines that think. We adapted. People always adapt. These machines were sort of fun and useful, after all. Now the screens and machines and towers and satellites are everywhere, sprouting up like mushrooms in microwave manure. They keep tabs on where we are and who we are. This is an unprecedented situation. Nothing has ever occurred like this in the history of our race, and nothing will occur like it again. This is the defining moment of our relationship with technology.

Even as our art and music and our free thinkers and often our gut feelings warned us to be careful of these computer thingamajigs, we shuffled on board the Titanic Two, sailing into the unknown waters of the digital sea. Sure, now and then we got a little uneasy watching the kids being sucked into a fake reality; jamming their joysticks, virtually murdering and mutilating the replicating rows of cartoon phantoms. We saw "that look" in their eyes, the hint of slobber in the corner of their mouths. There certainly are some unsavory alleys in virtual game land- but, hey, kids will be kids.

Soon those kids were all grown up and they are the ones designing the new machines. Faster, farther, deeper, stranger.

How did this happen so fast? With so little conversation? We signed on for a three-hour cruise and pretty soon we're castaways on a virtual Gilligan's Island. Now the machine's saying "Hey, little buddy" all the time and Ginger wants your credit card number. Free time finds us screaming, "I am somebody!" into a toxic binary ocean where being somebody is a matter of opinion, to say the least. It is one machine now, so close to defining the human race. Turn away for a second. Take a breath.

There is one natural reality. It didn't hide its intentions from us. Natural reality never kept tabs on who our "friends" were, never paraded non-stop virtual violence and hyper-sexualized madness in our children's faces. It didn't corrupt and destroy traditions like they were made of toilet paper. Natural reality didn't herd us away from our old social gathering places. It didn't sell us our musical heritage from a centralized database. Natural reality didn't outsource our jobs or make us pale and dumb and give us phony news 24-7. Natural reality didn't GPS our locations or take pictures of our house for its map. It never obliterated our time by making us run faster and faster like we're part of a hamster-wheel "video experience" instead of a human tribe. Natural reality never scanned us or chipped us or watched us or catalogued us or cloned us or created robot replacements for us. Natural reality gave us a place to thrive. It did not condemn us to a doom without dignity.

There's a creepy-crawly feeling that's been going around. Something's not quite right about where this show is headed. Maybe you think I'm out of my mind. No matter. Maybe you should keep reading anyway. Maybe you're supposed to read these words. Isn't that how it all works? Maybe the time has arrived in this shared dream for riddles and coincidences, ironies and paradoxes...even punch lines. Maybe you get it. Maybe you realize nobody's got all the right words to say this kind of thing, but you're willing to hear me out.

Let me get this out on the table. I'm no Unabomber, folks. If there's anything that truly repulses me, it's violent people. I'm no politician either. I don't have any laws to pass. I'm no scientist, with studies and pie charts and diagrams and test tubes to prove my points. I'm no professor, with my doctoral thesis all neatly researched and referenced. I'm no professional conspiracy theorist, who assumes that anyone with a scary campfire story deserves a hysterical hearing in the semi-public eye. Sure, I'm a bit of a storyteller. But hey, who isn't?

I'm not making this stuff up.

Still, I do think this whole business is rather funny, in a way- all the robots and talking computers and brain scanners and gadgets and clones. Wow, it's just like they said it was going to be! Still, where is my jetpack? Where's my free time? Beam me up, Scotty.

I'm just a rather red-blooded working class American, and being an American means a lot to me. My folks have shown up for every war we ever fought. Freedom is always on the line in this world. But bullets can't win this war. They would only make our situation worse.

They can call me a fool, a hack, a fear-monger, a killjoy, a bore, a techno-traitor, a stick in the digital mud… or worse. I don't care. But hey, if you don't mind a brief interruption to our breathless cyber-love affair, then maybe you'll check out what I'm saying. Just because I have the nerve to say it doesn't mean I think I'm special. I don't claim to be a genius or prophet or preacher or pundit-but I'm no fool, either-at least not about this.

Screens, and the force which lurks behind them, are unhealthy to us on the deepest level- the level of consciousness, spirit and soul. Screens condition us to willingly accept being melded with machinery or controlled by machinery. The computer network will be used against us unless we take a deep breath and one relaxed step back right now. It's best to treat it like you would a grizzly bear, a snake or any other predator. Back away slowly.

First off, it's obvious that the digital network is being used to increase the power of run-of-the mill earthly tyrants. Okay. That's fine. I'm letting any and all of you run-of-the-mill tyrants know right now that I don't care to pick a fight with you guys. You can have the power, okay? It's yours. Tyrants are bad news, to be sure, but they aren't the worst of our worries. At the end of the line waiting for this machine to be fully installed is The Big Tyrant. You can't put his face on a wanted poster because he looks like nothing, like darkness. He's an It, a shadow that follows the human race around. He gets called by a lot of different names.

Of course, the new technology also does us favors. It's amazing, awesome and totally super neat-o! It's entertaining, informative, and creates "community". It's convenient for business, communication, travel and viewing sexy pictures of hot starlets. Everybody knows that the computer network is the greatest thing since sliced bread. It's very handy. I'm no "Luddite", whatever that is. I'm not saying we need to go back 200 years. I don't care to split hairs or argue with anyone about obscure points. There's not enough time to tip-toe around the holographic tulips. This thing eats freedom. It won't care how smart, holy or hip you are. It gives no regard to religion, economic status, cultural position, race or age. It corrupts consciousness. Consider taking a step back.

Once you've stepped back, you can just laugh at it. It's not even real-just a lie, a shadow, a mirage, a weird dream within a dream within a very real thing. What can you say? It just is what it is. What was the bad guy's disguise at the end of the story? Robbie the Robot! Ha! Good one. We should have seen it coming.

"I would have gotten away with it too, if it hadn't been for you meddling kids."

Welcome back to your story, my friends. It's either time to pray hard or party down, depending on your persuasion. Either way, I wouldn't recommend signing up to any new social network sites. Your new best friend there is the same old Big Brother.

Internet. Enter Net. Is this some kind of cosmic joke?

Did we say to our fellow fishes as we swam in the ocean of life:

"Hey! Check it out, guys, here's a big NET! And, look, there's a sign that says: ENTER! Net? Enter? Well, don't just float there, let's go on in!" ?

Folks, what happens when you enter a net or a web? Doesn't something come along and eat you? It advertises itself as the trap it is, making us spiritually complicit by our own comical naiveté -like we're the dumb guy in some cartoon. Something wants to show how stupid we are. We're not stupid, folks-just gullible. We were gullible to believe that our priests and philosophers and singers and scientists and politicians and journalists would warn us before we got into a situation as truly dangerous as this one. But they didn't warn us. They didn't because they were too busy surfing the web, just like we were. It's been a real surfing safari, folks. Surf City, here we come.

The Internet is the Beast.

My name is Sand and I hope you read these words. I'm a real person, not a pseudonymous blogger. I've had an interesting life- small town raised, college educated, ranch-hand and horse wrangler, landscaper, wildland firefighter, country and western entertainer for many years, vaudeville performer as of late. I've got lots of records (pardon me, CD's) if you want to buy one, but that's not why I'm writing this.

I'm writing this because ten years ago I watched the mountain named Mesa Verde in Colorado burn all night and I fell asleep beside it. I guess I must have had one hell of a dream-because when I woke up, everything felt and looked different. That was July in the summer of 2000. Shortly afterwards, I joined a contract forestry crew and fought forest fires in Oregon and Montana. When I got back I wrote a long book called What the Fire Said. I printed about 40 copies of it in September 2001 and mailed them to friends, former associates and acquaintances. That book said the same things I say here but in a different way. It also said things that I don't feel are necessary anymore to get my point across. So I wrote it down differently this time.

I'm not a professional writer or academic, and haven't received any grants or funding from any organizations. I'm not affiliated with any religious organization, secret society, denomination or political party. I believe that violence should never be used to fight for the beliefs I express here. I believe violence works against us-both here and in any unseen dimension or afterlife. Even smashing a toaster goes against the spirit of this work. So please don't smash toasters or cell phones or hurt people or get nutty and then say you got the idea from me. You don't need to get weird, please. Nutty equals weak in times like these. It's the last thing we need. What we need right now is spiritual toughness and a peaceful reassessment of our situation. A moderate, measured, even mellow reaction is the only response that might work in our predicament.

I'm not here to give you religion, and I don't think we need any new religions. The ones we have work just fine. I have no way of knowing what you believe or who you are. We believe what we believe.

All I know is that I see fake fires multiplying on the land, dressed as screens. I've been trying to figure out how this puzzle fits together and what we can do about it. I don't cherish this role. I'd much rather fly below the radar. But really, is any one else out there saying what needs to be said? At least I showed up for the gig.

I'll try and keep it fun. How about this? I'll promise big results. I'm not kidding, folks. This is a financial planner, exercise book and self-help primer all wrapped up in one nifty package. Here's the pitch:

Feel better! Save money! Lose weight! Sleep more soundly!

Do it the "Less IT, more Fit" Way!

Just follow these simple suggestions:

1) Cut back screen time by 75%. Keep your kids away from screens as much as possible (except maybe for communal things like Saturday morning cartoons, The Wizard of Oz or big sporting events).

2) Begin referring to the Internet every now and then as "the beast" or "that thing" or "It" and mocking the screen on occasion, dismissing it to its face, maybe sticking your tongue out at it. Deride its influence. Call it creepy. Pay attention to how you feel when you do this to the screen. Does it feel like the screen's an entity? Like you don't want to offend it? Does it feel like it's watching? If so, repeat step #1. Don't worry, there's nothing in the screen. It's not alive.

3) Take yourself off Facebook, Twitter, Cyberprayer.com, Sexysingles.org etc... all those social network, chat type of things that demand your constant upkeep and input.

4) Take two walks a day and just be with natural reality; with whatever is around you in the moment, with love. Try to experience the now. Read good books (not so many screens). Sing a little, or a lot...out loud if you get the chance. Be sure and breathe. Relax.

5) When you feel drawn towards unnecessary interactions with machines, stop and go walking again. This is where the weight loss comes in.

You'll see results in one month, guaranteed. Soon you may even be feeling so good that you'll want to take the Internet completely out of your personal life and disconnect your cable service. Talk about savings! Not to mention peace and quiet.

Can I guarantee you'll lose weight? Well, maybe. My hunch is that you will. Can I guarantee that the Universe wanted you to read these words? Absolutely.

I say I heard it in the silence, prove to me it isn't so.

Here are 99 Theses for the Age of It, written in the spirit of old Martin Luther himself, bless his rebel heart. I'm duct-taping them to the door of The Digital Temple. As a matter of fact, I'm sticking this thing up right now, and I don't care if I wake the neighbors. We have given a brain and body to a cosmic predator that never had an earthly brain or body before. This "It" lays a trap for what we call consciousness or spirit. We have an opportunity to give thanks to the One who made us, protect our children, and defend nature both within us and around us. We can accomplish these goals in a peaceful and good-natured way. It's a very easy course of action. In fact, we don't really have to do anything to make a difference. We can just stop doing so much of something that might be exhausting us anyway. Why not allow my book to be your excuse for two weeks? Just say:

"Well, I'm trying out this new "no Internet diet thing"... that's why I haven't returned your e-mails."

See, I'm already helping out.

Moderation is the key. Follow the middle path. But in the end, there's absolutely nothing wrong or weird about just canceling your TV and Internet service if you feel like it. You'll save money and time and you'll feel better.

Defend creation. Preserve consciousness- all while saving money and getting some extra free time. Who knew fighting the good fight could be that easy or this much fun?

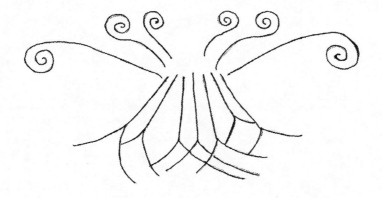

99 Theses for the Age of It.

PART ONE

Reality, Time, Fire and Story

Number One –Real is Good

Real is good. Whatever the substance might be of what we call reality, this substance is good and preferable to any computer simulation of that reality. Real is better than virtual. It is intrinsically better. It is eternally better. This is my assertion and my belief. If you think scientists and corporations can improve on the nature of reality, you are welcome to your belief. Personally, I don't think it's possible to improve on a tree, a star, a dolphin, a mountain, a baby or a woman. No virtual universe will ever come close to improving on reality. Nature is worthy of honor, both within us and around us. All heavily-funded efforts to alter our conception of reality should be viewed with skepticism.

The place we used to call the real world is inhabited by the energy form we call spirit or consciousness. There is no spirit or consciousness in the world of virtual reality. Nothing lives inside the machine and its programs. Nothing. The machine contains electricity and information, not spirit. All truth exists only in the realm of what we have traditionally referred to as the real world. An impossible position to prove? Hardly. One quick prayer or meditation will likely inform you of the same conclusion. The computer network is an alternate reality that completely lacks the presence of spirit, life, consciousness, or God. Real is the only real.

Number Two - Existence tells a Story with Time

This place called time allows for a notion known as story. We notice these stories, shape these stories and refer to these stories. All the peoples of the world have stories to provide meaningful explanations for their existence and how to behave. Religions have stories. Nations have stories. Social groups have stories. Families have stories. Individuals have stories. Story comes with the territory of consciousness. Any attempt to eliminate story simply results in new stories. Even science tells its own story under the guise of independent observation.

Reflection on the shared story of existence reveals cosmic or spiritual elements to this story, unseen forces affecting the land of appearances. We accept this unseen force, and offer it various titles, usually one of our names we have for the idea of God or the Creator or Spirit. But we also call unseen forces the Universe, Consciousness, Being, coincidence, synchronicity, fate, luck, mystery etc…Quantum physics has introduced the idea that observation apparently affects the process as well, which seems an important idea however one wishes to take it.

This Universe appears to be set up in such a way as to encourage story. Time, space, life, light, geographic and climactic elements, the presence of oxygen and water, the way the human mind works, all provide strong circumstantial evidence that this place called earth is home to a story.

Number Three - There are universally recognizable elements to all stories.

Stories contain characters, setting, plot, tension, and typically, a climax. We can't avoid this way of perceiving existence and truth. We are born storytellers and story-dwellers. Even our most mundane description of the day's events takes on story form.

Even science tells stories to impart its views to common

folk. Data and theory become interpreted in the form of story.

Here's a story:

"and then one day we came down from the trees and walked on two legs".

It's a story with tension (will they adapt?), a hero (the apemen…that's us, I guess), villains (the natural predatory order, extinction) and a climax (then we became people!!) Scientific discoveries are often told in story form…"and then Galileo saw the rings of Saturn" or "and then Pasteur made the vaccine!" or more recently- " then the Bomb stopped the war" or "then we made robots to help mankind."

Stories are a universally accepted means of imparting and sharing truth. We tell them all day, everyday. Stories can only be interpreted, however. They can't be "proved" in the classic sense. Things you can "prove" cease to be stories. If I drop a rock, it will fall to the ground. This statement can be proved, but it's not much of a story. "The universe started with a Great Big Bang" is a story that can't be proved, but still sounds like a pretty good story.

Stories that achieve lasting favor tend to address conflicts between love and hate, freedom and slavery, wisdom and ignorance, courage against the elements, good and evil, or a personal battle between one's own weakness and will. Think about a story that you love (whether it's Snow White, The Bible, or Jaws 3) and you'll likely find it residing in these patterns. Perhaps I'm just stating something obvious, but there's a point here.

Stories are how we understand existence. Whoever or whatever controls the storytelling process controls our relationship with truth. The new visual technologies are storytelling technologies.

Number Four - We are handing our story over to the new technologies.

Consider the old ways of storytelling that are on the way out: the campfire story, newspapers, theater, record albums, paintings and sculptures, books, puppet shows, sing-a-longs, live music...

Much of our knowledge, culture and music has been hastily handed over to a global system that could be rendered worthless by one good solar storm. The computer network has become the keeper of our shared human history. Written knowledge and recorded music not deemed worthy of "digital conversion" simply disappears into the dustbin of history. In the last twenty-five years, we have taken part in the greatest destruction of collective knowledge and art that has ever occurred on the planet. Whatever cannot or will not be converted into digital has become obsolete. Look at the piles of records, cassettes and books littering every garage sale and dumpster in America. Do we assume all that music was put on CD? Most of it was not. Those records selling for 25 cents are often some of the last remaining copies of that music in the world. How about those books no one reads anymore? Isn't it possible they had something to say?

The new technology is an information technology. We adapt our ideas of cultural memory to its capacity for data storage, what it loosely calls "memory". The technology then either erases cultural memories that came before it or adapts them to the network. By the nature of its high-speed format, it also sabotages attention spans, leading many people to not even want to read a book or listen to an entire record album anymore.

Our music and our story is being contained and delivered

by a machine. That machine's grip on our wisdom and culture gets stronger every day.

Number Five- Life in Reality encourages imagination.

Life in the place we used to call the real world encourages imagination. Life in the digital age hinders the development and use of imagination. Does a child who plays video games have as rich of an experience as one who plays outside with other children? Which boy is more creative: the one who learns to play guitar or the one who learns to play the Rock Star Video Game?

Has our music or popular culture or children's playtime improved drastically since the arrival of the Internet and video games? If so, then why do things often seem a bit like a rip-off these days? Sometimes it appears like there hasn't been an original cultural thought for decades. If ideas are original, they often come in the most prurient and despicable forms, as popular culture has apparently decided to push our boundaries of taste by pushing the boundaries of decency and dignity. That we even have a sub-category of film known as "torture porn" says volumes about our society.

Frankly, many of our people appear well on their way to becoming little more than button-pushing meat machines. Heads down, faces to their phones, thumbs-a-blazing; consuming like livestock in a drive-thru pen, entertained by the most unwholesome circus that ever came to town.

Imagination lets our minds grow and thrive. The digital age leaves very little to the imagination. I contend that this is not a healthy situation.

Number Six - We love Stories and Fires.

Stories are told around fires.

Once upon a time we sat around fires, stared into the flames and told each other stories. Then a box of flickering electricity came into our homes and upon our persons. Now we stare into this "fire" while it tells us the story.

This is the fundamental unspoken explanation for the acceptance and popularity of visual technologies-from the movie to the TV to the video game to the computer to the cell phone. We can't take our eyes off light sources that resemble fire. The human race accepted a relationship with visual technologies because of our trust in story and fire.

The ability to tell stories and make fires is a fundamental part of human character. The story around the campfire has been our heritage for thousands of years. We stare into the fire while someone tells us stories. This relationship came into the home with the hearth and fireplace. The hearth in the home was replaced as an altar about 60 years ago by a storytelling machine emanating crackling light. The storytellers of old were the ones that told us the truth. So we gaze into the new fire seeking the truth, and what do we see?

Number Seven - We are losing the ability to interpret basic riddles or read signs.

Having been force-fed a pseudo-scientific, non-meaningful explanation of the Universe, we lose the ability to interpret basic riddles or read obvious signs. We seem unable to understand simple historical patterns. The interpretation of information is left up to so-called "experts", who appear as commentators on visual technologies. We are so barraged by information that truth itself has become an anachronistic idea, something that folks used to believe in, perhaps in the "good old days". A society divided from any sense of its own history or cultural memory is inevitably being prepared for its downfall. It lacks the ability to learn from the mistakes of the past. It also lacks the authority to convincingly warn itself when elements of society are seeking new levels of power at the expense of the masses.

When Martin Luther spoke out against the Medieval Church's practice of selling indulgences (essentially tickets to heaven or "Get out of Hell Free" cards), he was simply stating that the practice was not Biblical or logical, and that there was an irony involved in doing something so preposterous.

When the Founding Fathers of America, undeniably rational men, decided to separate the colonies from England, they had no scientific "proof" that the idea known as freedom was necessary to the human condition. They founded the nation on principles that are difficult to define, yet universally recognized.

"We hold this truth to be self-evident, that all men are created equal…"

We seem unable these days to say that true freedom's even necessary, or come up with a definition of freedom that would be acceptable. We don't discuss in our schools whether basic privacy or morality is fundamental to a pleasant society.

In fact, we seem unable to communicate much of anything to anybody else these days. In the ultimate paradox of the information age, the ability to share unlimited information has resulted in the most uninformed population in history, a population that doesn't have the time to care about things as fundamental as their own survival, rendered mute and powerless even as we blog and tweet about everything under the sun.

Our most popular shows on TV star people whose private lives are exploited, where "reality" is re-defined as "show".

The most popular show on the Internet is pornography.

The most popular show in the world is the "social network" -where our lives become a show.

It just so happens that the real story (the one that happens in the place we used to call the Real World) is probably about truth and freedom. In that real story, there is a shadow Force that works in opposition to freedom and truth and love. Most of us suspect that such an "enemy" figures in the story of humanity. This suspicion of a "cosmic enemy" comes to us naturally, and is a universal phenomenon. Political, religious, and economic forces have always taken advantage of these natural suspicions by re-directing them at other religions, cultures, nations or social philosophies. This strategy works to cement power. Forces in power know the best way to create the tribal unity they need is to confront or invent an enemy. We would be fools to expect much truth from corporate or political forces engaged in the process of ruling and moneymaking. The installation of a vast international brain that rapidly takes over our lives should be looked at with heaps of skepticism- or at the very least, caution. But people are easily deceived. They love order. They love convenience and entertainment. They enjoy feeling important. They especially like magic tricks.

We have largely lost the ability to interpret basic messages and riddles about the world around us. You will re-discover this ability within a few weeks of canceling your internet and disconnecting your cable service, provided you walk out every day into nature and consider the real world that was given us free of charge.

Number Eight - Enter the Net. Or, if it's a World Wide Web, there must be a Spider.

Enter net. A prophetic pun. A mundane cosmic joke that proclaims its own punch line. It's supposed to be funny, I suppose.

What happens when you enter a web? Who is the spider?

Look at the fate of the fly.

Bugs don't get away with surfing webs for long. Why should we be different? A hundred years ago, schoolchildren would have laughed at what amounts to a nursery-rhyme testament to humanity's misplaced faith.

This isn't a human conspiracy. It's too odd and beautiful for that. Yes, people installed the network and profited from that installation. But in the end, it's not a human that intends to occupy this extraordinary tool of tyranny. It mocks us. A basic riddle.

Number Nine - WWW=666

In Hebrew, letters are also numbers. W, or the "va" sound in Hebrew, also stands for the number 6. This factual curiosity receives very little notice and, when it does, much derision. Still, it is the simple elegant truth that the 13th Chapter of the Book of Revelations in the Bible can be read as saying the "number of the beast" is www.

The Opposing View: Critics say the Bible says literally "Six hundred and sixty-six" rather than six, six, six. This translates to a different series of letters than www. True.

Nevertheless, when people refer to the mark of the beast, they nearly always say "six,six,six" rather than "Six Hundred and sixty-six". So the commonly used term for 666 does indeed translate to www. We're talking about a 2,000 year old vision received by a man (John) tradition says was left to die on a deserted island. If there are minor discrepancies in the rendering of semantics as he looked across the gulf of time, so what? When you say "six, six, six" in Hebrew, you say the equivalent of w,w,w. It's just that simple.

But as exhausted and brainwashed as we currently are, there is little guarantee that even this easily translatable tidbit might make much difference. Our current stock of media evangelists appears too busy making money, hating Muslims, aligning themselves with political profiteers, and building fancy websites to bother mentioning that the only thing you really need to worry about in the Book of Revelations almost certainly turns out to be the computer network, or at the very least will use that network to achieve its ends, whether you put stock in the translation or not. With souls on the line, with human spirit, nature, freedom and consciousness at stake, their cowardice is appalling.

Number 10 - Let's call it It.

It calls itself IT, Information Technology. I call it "It" too, but I'm not referring to the technology itself, which is a heap of wires, plastic and electricity. The real It is our old nemesis, the shapeless shadow on the human race that works through one side of our humanity to attack innocence, decency, nature and freedom. It has followed us around since the beginning. Some call this force a devil, but unfortunately such names often conjure cartoonish images, and this force is not a cartoon. Until now, the It operated on earth within the confines of the human mind, limited by our biology and human intelligence. Finally, it's apparently tricked us into giving it an earthly form and mind, so that it can shape the future of the human race. The It has begun to occupy the computer network.

Number 11 - It appears as an angel of light.

The It is simply a shadow, a lie, a formless fallen angel. But it can appear as an angel of light when we give it the power of electricity. The shadow glows. The angel of light that appears then appeals to our vanity, our boredom and our desires.

The digital angel, the magic man, the huckster, complete with new illusions-now in 3-D, all smoke and mirrors, kind of Las Vegas-y but not as fun. In spite of the reality that waits outside our door, we prefer the magic trick. The incredible variety of natural existence is ignored to look at a shiny fire box...

"It performs great signs, even making fire come down from heaven to earth in the sight of all; and by the signs that it is allowed to perform on behalf of the beast, it deceives the inhabitants of earth...and it was allowed to give breath to the image of the beast so that the image of the beast could even speak..."

From that dusty book that's lying around somewhere-
Revelations 13

It's not real light, just a parlor trick. Magic. Fire from "heaven".

Number 12 - A very real illusion, a story performed with spirit.

Well, what is real, then?

"I am not of this world", Jesus said.

"Look upon the world as you would on a bubble, look upon it as you would a mirage", The Buddha said.

This world, when examined under the most powerful microscopes, is simply vibrating energy that has no true shape. Matter is not matter in any way that can be truly defined. Solid is not solid. At the bottom of it all is what? An illusion? A dream? A story? Hindus have expressed something to this effect for centuries. In their cosmology, God has taken on all the shapes and identities in the "play" of reality- a fact these "characters" promptly forget lifetime after lifetime. Now, to be sure, the Jews and the Muslims have a different take on the reality of this place, as do you and I and everybody else.

But most of us agree on one thing: even if it is a dream, what goes on here matters. Sure, maybe it's an illusion, but it's a very real illusion filled with genuine elements such as love, sacrifice, family, friends and nature. Long ago, it became obvious to our ancestors that what we do in this lifetime resonates on an unseen plane. We defend our eternal soul by our earthly actions. We justify our ancestors when we behave bravely and with decency. We honor God by doing the right thing here on earth. This appears to be a story, and what's behind that story can't be seen or described. The physicists never get to the bottom of it, no matter how many new particles they discover. Only the mystics and the prophets seem able to approach the truth, and because of the constraints of language, they usually just leave us with riddles.

Number 13 - We believe in natural reality because consciousness is real.

We behave with a sense of morality instinctively, knowing that moral sense much as a bird knows its migration path. Consciousness is real and informs our existence. Particles may not have any substance, but consciousness and life do. Consciousness may be the only force that can be considered "real" in this situation. Consciousness can also be read as spirit or perhaps "soul".

Suppose a machine is allowed to trap consciousness by melding with the human mind and body. Suppose internal consciousness receives instructions from an outside source. Can there then remain any free will?

Furthermore, because of the nature of the relativity of time ("Past, present and future are an illusion, no matter how persistent" Einstein famously said), couldn't such a trap be "eternal" on some level? The prophet in Revelations is adamant about warning the inhabitants of a far-distant future. There's been plenty of tyrannies and empires enslaving us from time immemorial. Why would 666 be different? Perhaps because the It lays a trap not just for freedom, but for free will. It lures us into a subservient intimacy with a machine that lacks human characteristics like love or mercy.

This is unprecedented. All people should find common ground in addressing this threat. Consciousness, which exists simultaneously within time and beyond time, can be hijacked by this machine. We may very well be lured by promises of a virtual heaven and delivered to a techno-hell instead.

It is an inter-dimensional trap, crafted in predatory detail by a desperate cosmic architect. It is a prison masquerading as a dreamscape.

Number 14 - As history progresses, tyranny becomes more efficient.

Tyrannies are always popping up in one form or another. But every now and then, they evolve in fantastic new directions. Tyranny utilizes new technology in these periodic growth spurts.

From the domestication of the horse to the invention of wheels and guns, from the airplane to the Intercontinental Ballistic Missile, new technology not only makes life easier for some, but also advances the aims of empires. The efficiency of tyranny increases through history-just as the collapse of those tyrannies becomes more spectacular.

The Nazi empire only lasted from 1933 to 1945. Employing the latest advances in modern warfare, including primitive computing capabilities, they launched a well-coordinated assault on their neighbors, as well as on certain members of their own population. The Nazi war machine and social control systems were an extraordinarily efficient, and initially successful, operation. These efforts at establishing the fabled Third Reich would have been more successful had Adolf Hitler not been a neurotic, unstable man. His initial successes made him vain and hasty. He suffered from the paranoia that accompanies tyrants. He provoked war with Russia and America even though his armies were unprepared. He overextended his resources, missed numerous opportunities and left his nation vulnerable. This is the way of human emperors. The ego's mystique of invincibility is its downfall. In the end, Hitler was terribly defeated. 60 million were dead and Germany was in ruins.

There's always another empire just around the corner, and perhaps our beautiful world has become something slightly different in the wake of our successes. Still, human tyrants are just people. They can't take away our forever. They aren't what I'm worried about.

The efficiency of tyranny increases in history.

Number 15 - Mirror, mirror, on the wall. Who's the most efficient tyrant of them all?

He's the big Pharaoh, Fuhrer, Czar, Commander, Warlord, Darth Vader type…the shadow It. Operating through all tyrants, from the schoolyard bully to the King of Babylon, It seeks to prove that we are a beastly, petty and cowardly race- not worthy of the gift of free will. It seeks to provoke us with fear and terror into handing over our freedoms.

Each time, the It was surely disappointed in the earthly tyrants it trusted with its mission. They were fools. They made bad decisions.

The Tribe of Light was too strong for darkness to overcome, too attached to the ideas of freedom and justice. Liberty sprouted organically from oppression.

Now it's different. A machine will not think like a man, and is patient enough to wait until the net is full before it draws it tight, to keep still on the web it has spun. It is the perfect predator. Those who have made their livings installing the machine aren't to blame. They have no idea what they helped create.

Number 16 - The game is Diversity versus Monotony.

The "physical" Universe around us is the very definition of diversity. Diversity is not a dirty word, as some have tried to make it in the last few decades. Diversity is the very foundation of physical matter, the sustenance of life, the fruit of freedom.

The world of the It is the world of Monotony. The paved world. The Mega world. The secure world. The Big Brother says "watch your step" world. The microwaved pixilated streamlined unified world. A world that is watched on a screen and not lived in.

God loves diversity. Look at any forest wilderness.

What force desires monotony, unanimity, sameness? This is a simple riddle. We don't need any science to explain it for us.

Number 17 - Stories within stories within stories.

It's the story lodged in the bones of creation, written with free will and fate, a struggle between truth and lie, existence and non-existence. God, the source of the living dream, created it and participates in it for his own reasons.

But here's my pitch: a localized action has larger consequences, creating the basis for lessons to be learned. Along the way are tough decisions, great conflicts, and narrow escapes. Does it sound like the plot for a TV movie? Of course it does. It sounds like every plot line. Maybe the reason it sounds like a story is because we live in one.

PART TWO

The List of Boogeymen, The Spooky Show

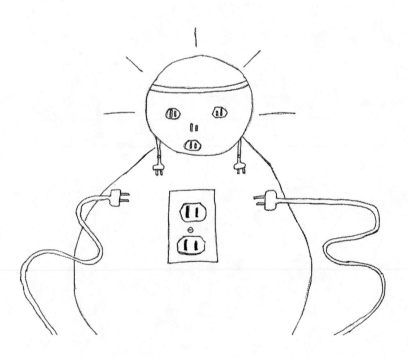

Number 18 - It's not about us adults. It's about future generations.

This isn't about you 30-ish hipsters with your I-pads and cappuccino buzzes sharing the "Cloud" with your virtual buddies. This isn't about Grandma sending e-cards and pictures to Sally and the kids. This isn't about Mr. Captain of Industry and his all-important laptop with those vital secrets and programs. This isn't about Sneaky Sammy and his 400 digital porn shops. This isn't about Social Network Betty and her countless virtual friends, her endless chatter and twitters and postings and tags, her life outside of life; her dream parade. This isn't about you and how you've decided to spend your time. That's your business. Just like whatever I do should be my business. This isn't about you or me.

It's about the world we prepare for our children. At what point does the digital dream turn into a nightmare? 10 years? 25 years? At what point do we face this? It is common knowledge that creatures become "adjusted" to intolerable, even deadly conditions by the gradual introduction of those conditions. You can boil frogs alive in a pan without them jumping out by simply starting them off in cool water and slowly turning the heat up. We become adjusted to the insane demands of modern life by gradually adjusting to them. We adapt. That's what people do.

Our children might adapt. But part of them cannot survive the adaptation to the future world of this technology. This is not about us adults and the choices we had the freedom to make. It's about the distinct possibility of creating a world where there will be no choice. Do we want that as our legacy?

Number 19 - There are immediate and long-term threats to our freedom and survival coming from the field of robotics.

It's not my intention or desire to make a comprehensive list of the various heartburn-inducing advances in the field of robotics. A ten second Google search will tell you all you need to know.

As I write this, Predator Drone aircraft are monitoring US borders, marking the first time any nation has patrolled itself with robots.

Robots are being tested as teachers in Japanese schools.

Robots have already eliminated millions of jobs.

Scientists have developed self-replicating robots, able to make perfect copies of themselves, even on the molecular scale.

Robots are becoming an established weapon in armed forces around the world.

Robots have been developed that devour flesh to power themselves (the slugbot). A real gift to society, that one.

Antbots have been developed that can organize themselves.

They have created robots for sex. The inventors claim we'll learn to love them just like we would human partners. What will we buy them on Valentine's Day? A new power strip?

They developed a robot snake even, soon to be slithering out of a hole near you.

It doesn't take a genius or a paranoid to see that robots which can replicate themselves, find and metabolize their own sustenance, and learn the tactics of warfare pose a threat to the freedom and survival of the human race.

Now they even want to send robots into space, so they can spread like a life-eating cancer across the universe.

Number 20 - There are other threats developed in the name of security.

There has been rapid development and implementation of various security and identification technologies, here in America and also abroad, often in the name of the so-called "war on terror".

No sense me listing everything. Information is readily available in much greater technical detail elsewhere. But here are a few of the things we've seen introduced:

Cell-phone eavesdropping, e-mail interception, the widespread cataloguing of Internet activities. GPS tracking.

Routine searches. Video surveillance. Body scanning. The brain scanner- which I suppose knows whether you are telling the truth or not.

Microwave weaponry. Great, just after they put up all those towers everywhere. At least we can heat up our burritos for free now.

The push towards universal identification. RFID. Iris scanners. Biometric id's. The beginnings of micro-chipping (pets, then convicts, then children).

Rumors of bizarre weapons and devices straight out of a science-fiction book, designed by scientists on the payroll of various international war machines…weather control, electro-magnetic weapons, mind control…the spooky show accelerates like a carnival ride, and the carny's in a mask.

All these bad dreams will turn to dust some day.

Number 21 - We are becoming like Lab Rats, looking for rewards.

As has become apparent to any number of researchers and social observers, the Internet has led us into an obsessive-compulsive relationship with technology. We can't wait to check our e-mails. We can't wait to get new Tweets. We feverishly anticipate new messages and our responses. Gotta check it. Gotta check it. Gotta check it.

The idea of getting a new message becomes what the idea of a piece of cheese is to the rat in the cage. We fixate on the possibility of new e-mails and Facebook postings like a Labrador fixates on a tennis ball. The reward is information, or a sense of importance. Though this process may not be deeply satisfying, we repeat it anyway, endlessly, every day, often pathologically.

And now, a portable screen for everybody.

As if the idea of reality wasn't under assault enough, the last ten years have brought the onslaught of the portable screen, the constantly connected mobile distraction. The vision of a free-willed people with their heads down, turned away from each other and reality, seeing the world through the lens of the It.

What would past generations have thought if they could see us? We appear a little bit "off our rocker", even kind of pathetic. Dehumanization is not pretty.

Number 22 - Reality TV prepares us to be watched.

Reality TV and "you tube" get us used to the idea and the process and the feeling of being watched. This idea, which appeared benignly at first as "funny home videos", later morphed into watching people being filmed against their will on "Cops". You Tube offered us an easily accessible video network which has now evolved into real-time video streaming on the web at any time from cameras positioned anywhere. We have become each other's show.

In spite of occasional "positive programming", visual technologies have come to specialize in showing us at our worst-as fools and victims, clowns and connivers, as sex-crazed rats in a rooms-to-go cage. Two-dimensionalized into caricature, we watch our own public embarrassment, episode by episode.

With names like "Big Brother", "Survivor" –even "American Idol", at least this thing has a pretty good sense of humor-more than we can say about much of America. Do we like to watch other people's humiliation and misery?

"Sure, sort of," comes the repellent answer.

Number 23 - The TV and Internet are filled with grotesque content.

The real problem with visual technologies and the digital age is form, not content.

Still, as Jesus said:

"You will know them by their fruits."

Flip through the channels about 8 o'clock tonight. What's on the tube? Murder, gore, rape, torture, hyper-sexualization, dumb game shows, unfunny comedy, hypnotic lights, inane "reality" shows, noise, bells and whistles, hoarders and hustlers followed by video cameras into the dark alleys of their private lives, then more murder, murder, murder. Then commercials for more shows about murder and demon possession and new gadgets to watch those shows on. It's Rome with less shame. We out-babylon Babylon. Maybe it's time to have the service disconnected. The few good nature shows, sports and interesting stuff that remain are simply not worth the trouble and expense anymore. You can always go watch the big game at somebody else's house, or even at the bar, which at this point, is probably healthier than having visual technologies in your house.

Some true art still manages to get through to us on the screens. Some fun stuff is out there, but look at how much isn't fun or nice or even remotely decent. Americans average between four and eight hours a day with the television on and most of the time they'll be the first to admit it's mostly garbage.

Number 24 - Video Games.

Take five minutes and watch a child with a video game. Staring hypnotized, slobbering over the machine- lured into another reality by pulses of phosphorus light. Children who should be picking dandelions, looking at clouds and playing with a ball are turned into jacked-up techno-vegetables.

Virtual Reality is the ultimate lure of the force that confronts our traditional reality. Virtual Reality promises to make us gods of our own universe. The prophets of this technology promise us that soon, we will be fully immersed in that virtual reality. When that happens, they say, we'll be unable to distinguish the virtual world from the place we still call the real world. They say we'll be able to plug virtual reality directly into our brains. Who will be telling the story then? When we attempt to download paradise into our brains from a ubiquitous Internet Cloud, will it be paradise that is delivered?

Virtual Reality: the fake war, the fake woman, the fake hero, the fake story, the fake thrills, the fake life…

It's a trap.

Let's put these damned joysticks down for a minute and consider this situation.

Number 25 - Nanotechnology is insanity.

Nanotechnology: self-replicating molecular machinery that can make virtually anything out of anything else. Will the universe tolerate the reckless reconstitution of the building blocks of matter? Who is in charge of such activities? Did we really need this type of technology to live well on earth?

Number 26 - Synthetic life and cloning are abominations.

I do not recall anybody clamoring for the invention and widespread use of cloning. I do not recall our society being in poverty due to a lack of clones. Synthetic life is even creepier. To change us from the inside out as the machine comes at us from the outside in. Defying nature, God and common sense in an all-out assault on the boundaries of reality.

Your designs, Doctor Frankenstein! Where is the love in your work?

Remember Dolly the sheep? They made four more of her now. Who does she belong to now? Does she look across the pen and see herself in the eyes of her replicated playmates? Why did they choose a lamb to do this to? Will they ever let her die?

Number 27 - Servant or master?

The growth of computer intelligence leads us to assume a subservient role to our own technology.

"Head to the Cloud!" they say on the commercials. We are supposed to celebrate being brought together inside the soul of the network.

Computers become more intelligent exponentially over the course of history. This apparently true theorem is known as "Moore's Law", which dictates that the processing power of computers (the amount of transistors per chip) doubles roughly every two years. Computers are able to download information directly into other computers, which allows them to "learn" in ways and at rates humans are incapable of.

Computers now connect into what is apparently becoming a single unbroken interface. First the Internet, then the "Cloud", then…

What will replace "The Cloud"? The prophets of the Digital Age predict a thing called the Singularity, when the computer network alters us into something no longer recognizable as humanity. They foresee computers and natural reality somehow congealing into a seamless mass. They predict the ability to download our consciousness into the machinery. They see this in the next 50 years, not the next 500. I do not wish to explain their dream here, just as I'd rather not speculate on the reality of hell. Punch in Singularity on the search engine and it will tell you more than you care to know.

Will the creative power that made the dolphins and the human spirit and the redwoods watch passively as they are consumed and replaced by a digital dream? What is to become of our children in the Singularity? Who will run the Singularity? Someone that we trust? Let's not fool ourselves.

Number 28 - It is a Tracking System.

The advent of GPS, RFID(Radio Frequency Identification), satellites, and ubiquitous microwave towers allow for the physical tracking of nearly anyone at a moment's notice. We are on the verge of literally having nowhere to hide. I suppose this would be fine as long as we trust our authorities, but sometimes, well, ...you get the picture.

" Why are you worried about us searching if you have nothing to hide?" has been the mantra of tyrants for millennia. It is precisely why our Founding Fathers prohibited unreasonable search and seizure in our Constitution.

Besides that, nearly everybody leaves an easily-traced digital trail these days. Our purchases are catalogued, our e-mails collected, our surfing noted, our friends inspected and listed, our favorite websites stored until every individual presents a unique "virtual" identity. The mainframes are plenty big enough to maintain such files, and more importantly, the computer network is intelligent enough to sort through such mountains of digital dross to assess who is a "threat" to society and who isn't.

For an example, meet John Doe. He's a "regular" guy. The computer network "knows" that John Doe maintains ties through Facebook with old high school friends who ended up in trouble with the law. From his on-line purchases it determines that he likes hunting. From following his surfing it registers that he reads certain "conspiracy" websites regularly and that he listens to and downloads "anti-social" heavy metal music. His "anonymous" comments on the Internet show an anti-authoritarian perspective, and these comments are catalogued because his computer, like all computers linked to the Internet, leaves a unique fingerprint. To top it off, sometimes late at night, when his wife and kids have gone to sleep, John Doe looks at a wide variety of graphic pornography. This is also duly noted, perhaps with a cyber snicker from the mainframe.

The network sees all this. It writes it all down on a virtual list. It organizes and edits and makes files for possible use at some later date. It's the digital Santa Claus. It sees you when you're surfing. It knows when you're awake. It knows when you've been bad or good so …you know the rest. This is not paranoia, just simple fact. Human beings in the law enforcement community do not typically monitor such electronic affiliations and movements. That is impractical. But the machine can gather and edit this information automatically.

Should we put John Doe on a list of folks we need to "watch out for"?

There's reason to believe John Doe is already on such a watch list, a list so comprehensive that no human could possibly sort through it- only the computer itself is capable of editing such a mess. It's not hard for a computer to do. Say you need a guide to well-armed potential troublemakers. Do you have access to the servers? Well, if you do, just punch in a few key words to the mainframe… let's say "freedom" "guns" " survival" with a couple readouts of who goes to which websites…throw in some already suspicious associates. Do this and you would probably have a decent roughly edited list of potential enemies of the state. They were found by utilizing the computer's amazing ability to cross-reference. We use the same technique on Google every day. In the near future, the computer will create the list of suspects. The computer will weigh "the evidence". It's even possible robo-cops and drones will carry out its "justice".

There are probably many people in America who would already agree that our imaginary subject John Doe should be viewed with suspicion, even if he's committed no crimes, simply because of his opinions and associations. With the advent of the preposterously abstract "war on terror", suspicion and fear have become our new national pastime. Perhaps that's why you see such an effort these days from people trying to posture themselves as more patriotic than their neighbor.

There are many possible means of keeping such "enemies" as John Doe in check with minimum expenditure of energy and manpower. The first and foremost method of social control involves the addictive nature of the web itself. The Internet simply keeps these "anti-social" people so busy blogging and complaining and surfing and "friending" that they rarely do anything in the real world anyway. Most of them remain virtual rebels, so concerned with maintaining their "anonymous" digital identity that they'd never actually hold up a picket sign in public; much less perform some physical act of sedition. They just leave obscenity-strewn "comments" on cyber-news items, so that you'll know how angry they are. The connections they maintain, the community they inhabit, is a mirage. They never truly get together with fellow believers. They know each other only through the de-personalizing, utterly non-existent "cloud". Becoming angrier and more disenfranchised all the time, the computer exacerbates their anti-social tendencies.

Another way to maintain social control in the digital age is through the fear of exposure. In the back of John Doe's mind, he worries about all those embarrassing porn sites he visits late at night. He even feels a little guilty. Could that come out somehow? He's begun to suspect his visits have been catalogued. Could they be brought to the attention of the public and his family if he were to make a public personality of himself?

This is where the "idea" of the network works in concert with Reality TV, You Tube, camera phones and the like. We'll maintain and guard our own prison. We fear exposure in the public eye, even as we make our lives into more and more of a public show. We will keep the prison gates ourselves. We fear the network's apparent omnipotence as well as its great strength. This is a great clue about the nature of the "It". It operates in the opposite manner as the Creator. Its power is fear. It catalogues our secret sins and does not forgive them. Not only does it not forgive, it stands ready to share our failings and shames with the world if you dare to cross It. Look at these cameras in everybody's hands all the times. We all live one click away from immediate worldwide exposure. Worse, with access to Photoshop and other graphic manipulation tools, we can be placed in any fraudulent pose, associated with any manufactured sin or crime, no matter how preposterous.

The very idea of the computer can be used to invent crime. If someone in power has an enemy, just confiscate the "enemy's" computer, take it to "the lab" and claim your "experts" found kiddie porn or nuclear bomb plans in the hard drive. How would anyone know the difference if such material was really there or not?

It's all "virtual" evidence. It's like confiscating a brain and charging it with "thought crime". Such is the inherent danger involved in maintaining any relationship whatsoever with the technology of the information age. It's not surprising that fewer and fewer people feel like "rocking the boat" when it comes to age-old American ideals like freedom and justice. We are already deathly afraid of the It-a fact which It loves, if It's indeed capable of love.

Number 29 - Al Gore did not invent the Internet.

The Internet was conceived in the womb of the war machine and sustained by our boredom, desire and vanity. Do a 5-minute investigation to follow the money behind the big search engines, the ones that have photographed and catalogued our entire planet. You'll discover that this is a social control system seeking your voluntary compliance. But that is the least of our worries. The profiteers and nerds who installed the network have no idea that the real master of the machine still lurks in the shadows, waiting for his turn to be a You Tube Star, to bring the Yahoos and Twits into His Space.

Number 30 - Melding Man and Machine is spiritual madness.

First microchip the pets, then the criminals, then the kids. Go bionic. The melding of man and machine. Sounds kind of cool until you begin to consider who might be holding the joystick that will run you around.

I heard a "liberal" commentator a couple of months ago mocking those afraid implanted microchips could be the mark of the beast. The "liberal" commentator works for the same machine (MSNBC, in this case…the MS stands for Microsoft) as the "conservative" commentators. These talking heads will all tell you to chip your kids when their boss says to.

Folks, let's not chip the kids. I bet they'd rather be a chip off the old toboggan than have one stuck in their noggin.

Number 31 - We do have a choice.

Technology may have helped us to evolve our brains, but it doesn't have to evolve independent of our wishes. Can it spur evolution? Sure. But certain technologies can also attack and disrupt healthy lines of social and biological evolution. Ask any tiger or whale- or Native American, for that matter. But technology is not some evolutionary progression that has to be followed to the bitter end. We have a choice.

Stepping back doesn't have to be spooky or scary. Just reduce your screen time by 75 %. It's as simple as that. Take your kids off the screens and cell phones and go take a walk at the park. Go swimming. Read a book (off a page, not a screen). Watch the sunset. Go breathe somewhere. Just because something was invented doesn't mean we have to get used by it, to buy it, to hand over our time to it, to be owned by it. We can be active, content, and even prosperous, - all the while maintaining limited interaction with information technology.

Number 32 - The god of Science lacks a code of Morality.

Science has become like a god, and technology provides the idols. We seek protection by the hand of this god, science, and look to it for our civilization's salvation. This god of science derives its authority from mystery, miracle and magic, just like all the other gods did. We beg the priests of this god for solutions to the problems science itself created.

Obviously, scientists aren't bad people. This should go without saying. On the contrary, scientists are just like the rest of us. The ranks of scientists are as diverse as humanity itself. Most science is either quite positive or at the least, benign. People who study frogs and light and stars and disease aren't doing anything wrong. They are nourishing human curiosity and seeking knowledge to help us.

Science became trusted because it made our lives easier and longer.

The problem is that science as an idea offers a belief system outside the realm of morality. It is a place where there is no divine judge or laws that relate to proper behavior. Science as an idea can then be used as an excuse by those in power to avoid morality, to ignore traditional ideas about the meaning of existence, ideas that imply we should do things like love our neighbors or take care of the poor.

Science is not impartial or objective. It errs on the side of omission. By its nature, it must disregard spiritual and circumstantial evidence, refusing to consider certain ideas we consider truths or common sense. Science is a tool. Its use has enlightened us and made our lives easier in many ways. But science shouldn't be expected to provide a moral compass to our lives. That's not the point of science, and never has been.

Political and economic forces often take advantage of scientific amorality to insert their own agendas. Adolf Hitler was not particularly religious, but was instead devoted to the "science" of eugenics. Holy books typically say we should avoid violence and share wealth with the poor. Science won't even say that, and even if it did, this stance can only be stated as a position, not as a "truth".

When the reckless foreign company spills oil on our shores, we are told the problem will be studied by experts, the evidence weighed and conclusions reached. Justice often seems arbitrary. People end up in jail longer for breaking traffic laws than for poisoning the earth. The letter of the law is often followed to the exclusion of common sense. Urgent problems are not addressed. What is right or wrong is unavailable for discussion. This is a direct result of basing our civilization on a pseudo-scientific ideal propped up by bureaucracy.

Science isn't immoral. For instance, we are grateful for the efforts of the medical profession. But science alone isn't enough to save us. We need to save nature itself, both within us and around us. Looking at nature pictures in National Geographic won't be enough. We need to save the creation, life, free will. These things are truly at stake, no matter how many white lab coats might be trotted out to refute me. As cloning began to occur, which of our scientific friends took meaningful steps to stop it in its tracks? Maybe a handful. We need more scientists to speak up against pseudo-scientific adventures that threaten our future.

Science, lacking a universal code of morality, allows certain elements loosely affiliated with their community to sell technology to the highest bidder. The result of this well-known fact has come finally to threaten our existence.

Number 33- The modern age is letting us down.

The sky is filled with eyes that search your old secret spots. The microwave towers reach higher and further. Cameras are everywhere. Clones and robots aren't just in the movies anymore. Self-reproducing little machines scurry around in the molecular dust while nuclear missiles still chafe in their silos. The science fiction slaughterhouses fatten the population on genetically designed animals and plants. We live with vague and ominous warnings of Biological and Chemical warfare. Our food is stuffed with bizarre ingredients from anonymous laboratories. On a thousand channels at once, we watch the installation of the digital interface, then see the results on the street, the faces of our people staring down at their phones. The depressing submission of Internet and video game addicts. The extinction and degradation of the earth's creatures and wild spaces. The hyper-division and subsequent acceleration of time. The corruption of children's innocence. How dare we force these screens in their little faces? How can we possibly think it's ok to do so? How much longer are we supposed to suppress the notion that this is some kind of perverse plot?

Then people are going call me a fearmonger because I say it's better to go outside and breathe and sing and play in the open air and maybe even pray to God?

Who is our god now? Who do we believe controls our future? Who do we serve?

Number 34 - Maybe new Technology has stopped being our friend.

Hey, we all loved the light bulb and the radio and the car and the tractor and the blender and the refrigerator and the movie ... but the really important new stuff isn't coming anymore. We've received the things we needed most. Sewer systems, refrigeration, antibiotics, anesthesia...we have those things.

Much of the new technology isn't necessarily much of a friend anymore. Most of it is information, surveillance, or genetic technology. How much information can we handle before we go nuts? How much surveillance will it take to make us feel safe? At what point will genetic technology make us no longer human?

Technology is an extension of the human mind which either improves our lives or doesn't. Just because life is more efficient or lasts slightly longer doesn't necessarily make life better.

Technology is not inherently neutral. Sure, maybe some technology is. A shovel is neutral. You can either plant a tree or knock somebody over the head with it. But a flesh-eating robot is not neutral. Its only purpose is horrifying. Much of the new technology is funded by a bloated war machine. It's not like any of this comes as a big surprise.

Number 35 - Scientific and scholarly warnings tend to go unheeded.

We've seen countless studies that show television is harmful to young minds. There are mountains of data indicating that violent video games encourage violence, and that an internet-based lifestyle is unhealthy to extremes. These studies are dutifully reported and appear every few weeks buried in the information avalanche. It is supreme irony that we can be warned extensively of our own society's corruption and cultural dissolution in the same news cycle that contributes to this process. These warnings are given a spot on the "news" roundup, right next to the story which tells us what Angelina Jolie was wearing on the red carpet. Where do you think our eyes will wander first?

Scientific and scholarly efforts to tell us of the threats posed by our digital devotions are surely well-intentioned. But since they appear as minor news items within the media of the information age, they mean little in the eyes of our exhausted populace. We seem to be left with no choice but to make spiritual/religious warnings outside the network. Religious warnings are highly dangerous, as they often lead to disastrous misinterpretations by simple-minded zealots. But if "rational" elements of society are unwilling or unable to defend us from our current suicidal tendencies, then for better or worse, religious movements will appear to do the job. They will serve their traditional role of altering the course of history. It is up to those who participate in such movements to keep them dignified, decent, sane and peaceful.

Number 36 - The Science of resisting the It.

Out there in this big world are brilliant minds with good ideas about what needs to be done. They can try and re-shape the Net into something other than a freedom-eating monster. These scientists are some of our best hopes. Systems need fail-safes and back doors. We need to be able to always have control over our machines. Certain dangerous avenues of technology may need to be abandoned altogether. These issues should be at the forefront of discussion in classrooms and conferences around the world.

Number 37 - They say "You can't stop progress."

We say "you can't stop progress" like it's a natural order. I suppose it depends whose progress we're talking about. Hitler's idea of progress was stopped, after all.

Will we still say "you can't stop progress" if the powers-that-be come to stick microchips or computer goo in our heads? You can already imagine them saying:

"These are for your own good. These innovations have been tested and found totally safe. They are needed for health and security."

In whom do we trust? Once we believed that our God ruled the universe and did with it as he pleased. Now we believe that science does. When the deal goes down, I intend to place my bets on the one who made this game in the first place.

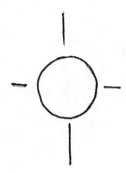

Part Three

The Construct and the Great Consolidation

Number 38 - We live in the Construct, but not in the Matrix.

There seems to be a contradiction here. Humans installed a bizarre tyrannical machine, but this is not a human conspiracy. How does that work? Well, you know the answer. It's not that different from building airplanes. An airplane can either be used to fly people home for the holidays or bomb villages into rubble. The folks who build the planes are simply making their livings building airplanes. The people who design the planes are simply being creative. Even the ones dropping the bombs are just following orders to protect their homelands. So how does neutral technology become non-neutral? How do good people become participants in creating unhealthy and/or aggressive societies?

Here's an effort at using a term: The Construct. But I'm not talking about the construct as it was used in the movie "The Matrix". Although I admit that film was pretty entertaining, I'm not into it. That movie's dream says we live inside a computer program, which is a load of bull. It says you must fight techno- tyranny with computers and violence, which is nonsense. That movie had its own line of video games, which tells us pretty much what we need to know about that movie.

The Construct I'm talking about is the world of money and power at work. It's the system that encourages the making of money and the gathering of power. Nearly all of us work in the Construct. The Construct rewards those who are most efficient at making money, and subjugates or eradicates those elements that do not serve its needs. It is a semi-conscious organism made of money, a living idea. Money flows though it as blood through a circulatory system.

Primitive and agrarian cultures have no place in the Construct. They are colonized or eliminated as the Construct becomes more efficient. If local natives can learn how to adapt, then perhaps their remnant population is allowed to live within the Construct. The Construct colonizes the minds of its subjects with desire for material success, and eliminates traditions that do not further the aims of the Construct.

The Construct also declares war on Nature, both within us and around us. The wildness and mystery of the natural order is replaced by an economic and technological order based on the material values of the Construct. Religions radically compromise with the Construct in order to maintain political protection and congregational support.

It is through the Construct that science became the universal belief system of our modern world. Science justifies a social system based on economic priority by cloaking life in non-moral terms.

The Construct strengthens its grip on power exponentially. Over the centuries it has used technology to "shrink" the world, becoming the dominant worldview across the various continents. Simultaneously it has hastened the collapse of the world environment. As the Construct expands, tribal systems falter and vanish- replaced by nations, and groups of nations. Tradition falls apart in the face of economic imperative and monocultural invasion. Independent cultural forces are tolerated only so long as they pose no threat to the Construct.

We are left with a unified consumer culture dishearteningly familiar to modern Americans-a dreamscape jammed with strip malls, mini-marts and fast-food outlets. We scurry along the conveyor belt of "life", looking at our phone for directions. We resemble links at the hot dog factory. We've gone so far as to microwave ourselves. Here comes the mustard.

An example of how the Construct works: rapidly drive out family farmers with underselling (much as Mega-Chains do small businesses) and then buy out their land. Two things are lost in this process: the tradition of the family farm and the tribe's ability to grow its own food. Food production and commerce is governed by a smaller and smaller group of corporations. They call it agribusiness. We call it unsettling.

Look how even drinking water can become a commodity.

The Construct creates dependency of the many on an elite few. This game is as old as the hills. It's just lords and serfs all over again. It is initiated with bribery and cemented with violence. I call the acceleration of this process through history The Great Consolidation.

Number 39 - The Great Consolidation.

Out of the raw market economics of the Construct arises the Great Consolidation, as society's means of sustaining itself become dominated by a shrinking list of multi-national forces.

We are becoming one world, but probably not in any grand spiritual sense. It's more like a plantation. The middle class is decimated. Skilled labor is eliminated by machines and outsourcing. We work for the company now, and if the company trucks stopped delivering food tomorrow, we would be in a hell of a bind. They could charge whatever they wanted for a loaf of bread, up to and including your soul.

The Great Consolidation is the real new world order,

oblivious to the politics that engage its member states. It is the last hurrah, the final manifestation of both Capitalism and Communism. It's not a bunch of creepy guys sitting around a table in some shadowy castle. It is the unconscious growth of a single worldwide economic organism, unifying itself so that the story which must be told will be told- finally, totally, truly worldwide. It smashes tradition, nature, privacy, decency, charity and religion to create a new faith, faith in It. Fear of It. The results? Absolute control- cemented and defended by the new universal machine that thinks.

Number 40 - The Construct encourages Desire.

The Construct, the power behind modern society, encourages desire- desire for material goods, social status and recognition, desire for sexual power. Desire is the fuel behind market economies. I'm trying to use the term "desire" in the same connotation as Buddha did when he called desire the root of suffering. In that sense, not meaning desire as a longing for improvement but rather desire arising from an unhealthy dissatisfaction with one's present state. We know the difference.

There is no end to the desire fueled by the Construct. These desires can't be fulfilled. They lead on and on into a house of mirrors. The constant comparison between one's actual status and an imaginary, unobtainable state of improvement is at the core of the "philosophy" of advertising.

This wallowing in desire runs counter to the teachings of every major spiritual philosophy. In the eyes of the prophets and mystics, such desire is the root of misery, anxiety, and violence.

Satisfaction with one's present lot in life is just that, satisfying. Peace might actually be attained when one isn't constantly thinking about what one doesn't have. But the Construct seeks to remind us that we don't have what we could have, what we should have, what others have. The result is a consumer society based on greed, lust and the quest for social prominence, an exhausting race towards a retreating mirage of happiness. This idea rots us from the inside out. The Construct keeps upping the ante with new products, new desires, new avenues to power and "satisfaction". Here's your new droid phone. Here's the new sex symbol-this time even younger, and wearing fewer clothes! Here's the new stock to buy or fast car to drive or greasy burger to eat or gadget to slobber on. Desire is the religion of the Construct and consumption is our common prayer.

Number 41 - The Construct controls the Story Now.

The Construct controls the story now. What does it say the story is about? Let's flip the channels and see.

After we wade through a toxic swamp of commercials, what do we find? Channel after channel packed with an astounding array of shows about murder and rape and torture and forensic specialists, ghoulish crimes both real and imagined. Keep flipping and you'll find acres of juvenile vulgarity in the form of obscene cartoons, inane sitcoms, screaming contestants on half-wit game shows, humiliating talent contests. Then we have the self-replicating "reality" shows…the sort-of acting, the dumb looks, the idiocy, the voyeurism. The Bachelor makes his choice on Temptation Island. The spectacle of people who think fame is worth this embarrassment.

Flip on over to the shopping network. Must…buy… stuff…Then to the food network. Must…eat…stuff… The history channel has no history on it. The music video channels have no music on them. The travel channel takes you nowhere but your couch. Lifestyles of the rich and fatuous. Check in on the suites of the elite. Oh look, a stray preacher with some random prosperity theology …oh good, he takes Discover!

Turn the channel and we find what is now called the "news". Seven channels of 24 hour breathless sensationalism complete with streaming banners updating us on the death tolls and the scandals, spotlighting red-faced political screeching matches, circular arguments howled into a high-definition hurricane. Talking heads in pancake make-up froth at the mouth with absurd allegations and phony dramas. We are inundated with disastrous information; assured that things are pretty much going to hell, and these goons promise to ride there with us.

That's the story, Construct style. And we actually pay them for this. We bring it into our homes, because we've accepted the premise. We sort of believe reality is in that box now. We have been conditioned to accept this story. The color box machine tells a story. We can't take our eyes off of it because it looks like a fire. Are we waiting for the truth to speak to us from the fire?

The truth will never speak to us from that fire. It is no burning bush. It is no Mt. Sinai. We are watching an electric shadow. Immersed in its cynical propaganda, we accept a degraded image of humanity as entertainment. Watch the pretty girl eat worms, watch the fat guy try and lose weight. Look at the hoarders, the jackasses, the Bachelorettes, the people stuck on the island. Who will screw over who to end up as "the survivor"? Send in the clowns. This is a perversion of the human story, a carnival mirror, a distortion.

We can just be done with it. Turn it off and cancel our "service". Some "service" that turned out to be. Go outside somewhere quiet and sit by the river, or under the trees or beneath the stars. We can just breathe deep the reality of true time, of spirit. Reality waits to take us back to peace in the here and now.

Number 42 -There is destruction of Nature within us and around us.

The Construct encourages the annihilation of the natural world and the annihilation of natural processes within our minds. We become more and more disoriented, farther removed from a balanced life lived within the laws of nature. This leads to widespread depression and mental illness. We take psychoactive drugs to hard-wire our brains into more readily accepting the new reality. Our minds work feverishly to adapt to the way of thinking and the worldview offered by the Construct.

We find ourselves racing to catch up with the latest demands of our technology. Now I need a cell-phone. Now I need GPS. Now I need internet-in the home, at the office, in the car, on my person...instant messaging, texting, tweeting. 3G network. 4G network. 100G network. More G's... please. And time (being just relative anyway) simply accelerates to match the demands of the new world. We live at an unbalanced, suicidal pace. To try and go any faster will require our total submission to mechanical time. I'm sorry, but this is not natural.

Number 43 – We have allowed the construction of a Debtor's Prison.

Having been encouraged to go into consumer and public debt, at some point the rug will be pulled out from us. Furthermore, society will soon operate completely on a "cashless" basis, as it very nearly does already. All our transactions will go through the computer network.

Revelations says:

"No one may buy or sell unless he has the…"

Mark my words, friends. Some prophecies in the Bible are bound to come true.

Number 44 - America the Hysterical.

We are pitted against each other in what amounts to political pornography. Blue against Red. Liberal against Conservative. The national media portrays our nation as a bloated bully scared out of his wits. Terror alerts. Full-body scanners. The joke that is computer voting. Hah, hah. Patriot Acts. The frothing hypocrite talking heads. Haven't they ever read the Sermon on the Mount? Or the Book of Isaiah?

"Woe to you who decree iniquitous decrees, and the writers who keep writing oppression, to turn aside the needy from justice and to rob the poor of my people of their right, that widows may be their spoil, and that they make the fatherless their prey! What will you do on the day of

punishment, in the storm which will come from afar? To whom will you flee for help, and where will you leave your wealth?"
    Isaiah 10

All political "sides" demand our privacy and dignity. All demand the shredding of our Constitution. Meanwhile the 24-7 hypnotizing of America marches on unimpeded. Left or right wing, it's still the Construct's Chicken.

Number 45 - The Binary Belief System.

Binary thought is 0's and 1's. Yes or No. And -Or -Not. There is no Maybe, no compromise with the unseen or supernatural. The Binary system is materialistic thought in a universe that isn't even made of material. All experience, history, art and music are plugged into this merciless equation, flattening our senses, removing wisdom and nuance and feeling. We become flatter and shallower by the minute.

Number 46 -The Construct manipulates desire for Security.

Benjamin Franklin famously said: "A society that trades liberty for security deserves neither."
    We seek order. We cherish security. We tend to trade freedom for order under the flimsiest of threats. Some folks will turn in their neighbors to the authorities in a heartbeat if they think it spares them from suspicion.
    Once liberty begins disappearing from the general population, the pattern continues until all liberty is removed from that population. Tools of tyranny are introduced as tools of security.

Enemies, both real and invented, are kept at the forefront of the news. Vague threats from strange forces allow for the introduction of stringent and invasive measures of security. The modern result? The self-guarded techno-prison, complete with body and retina scans, background checks and RFID's, microchips, brain readers, patriot acts. We lose the natural control of our own thoughts, bodies and movements that we once took for granted. Our desire for security is manipulated by political and economic interests. These interests are in turn manipulated by an unseen entity that can usually be found lurking in the shadows of the human story.

Number 47 - Institutions cannot be trusted with our Souls.

Institutions of earthly power-be they religious, economic, political, academic, scientific, cultural or otherwise-cannot be trusted with our souls. They cannot be trusted with our consciousness, with our spirit.

Can they be trusted to keep the lights on? Sure. To entertain us? It depends what's on the tube. Can we trust earthly institutions to look after the widows and orphans? Sometimes they do a great job. Do they pick up the garbage? As a matter of fact, they came this morning. Do they help bury our dead and build hospitals? Sure. We are blessed to have order in this world. It's great when institutions work. Order is a relief. Anarchy is miserable.

However, you cannot trust an earthly institution with your soul, or with your children's souls. There is simply too much at stake. There are also too many precedents for the failure of such institutions. Once again, take the example of our German friends.

Germans aren't bad people. Germany gave us Martin

Luther, Beethoven and Goethe, good beer and polkas. They'll jump in an icy pond as quick as anyone to save you. But in a few short years this last century, each of their institutions of power failed to protect the soul and spirit of their society. The Church stood aside during the genocidal rampage of the Nazis. The political system bowed to the dictator Hitler. The colleges were purged of critics. The scientists went to work building the machinery of war and terror. The culture began to reflect the designs of the Nazis and any art that dared criticize their reign was either ignored or crushed.

After the war, we hired surviving Nazi scientists and brought them here to help us build our computers and our bombs. It is all one grand march in history. We are not somehow impervious to laws of social reality just because we live in America. To assume so is reckless vanity. Americans are just as capable as anyone else of succumbing to the tender charms of tyranny in the name of order.

Earthly institutions of power cannot be trusted with your soul. Your soul is eternal. Your consciousness belongs to you and the eternal consciousness (that Force most of us call God). That's the real story. All this other stuff is just a big show. You don't have to believe in the infallibility of the state, and you don't have to be afraid of what some millionaire preacher screams about, or slobber over the earthly riches some self-help guru promises you. You don't have to agree with every scientific theory that comes out, or buy every technology corporate forces ram down your throat. You don't "have to do" anything because you were born with free will and you are of the eternal, and that's what those earthly forces want you to forget, because their power depends on your lack of power, and your fear of them.

Number 48 - We live under the Roman model of Power.

We live in a pseudo-scientific centralized society, a model left over from the Roman Empire. We live under the protection of an imperial state that colonizes primitive peoples, allowing them to nominally worship freely so long as the state's authority is not threatened by such worship.

Rome established a unified Church and colonized the European continent, leaving behind nation-states that proceeded to colonize the world. Look at our cities, our entertainments, our courts, our politics. We have inherited a society inclined towards materialism, justified by compromised, institutionalized religions. Our political structure claims to rule using a rationalistic, materialist, scientific view of the world.

That we are still generous and loving in the midst of this structure, and that our authorities are in general good to us, is a testament to this social model's effectiveness and to our collective decency. But we still live in Rome, make no mistake about it. We like a little bloodsport at the Coliseum. Somebody's always getting conquered or thrown in jail for not bowing to the emperor. We call it democratic even when it's really not, and religious when it's really not, just like they did. Rome: the pseudo-scientific, sort-of-rational, semi-democratic model of society. It's a model that works reasonably well, and I have no desire to change it. I'm just pointing it out because I think it's part of the riddle.

We live under the direct influence of the same state that conquered or slaughtered nearly every indigenous people in the world, that imposed an intolerant and brutal state religion for 1500 years, protected by the same generals that burned Jerusalem. We live in the same state that crucified Jesus Christ complete with the same hypocrites, now at different pulpits, patronizing and placating the same political celebrities who grease the same machine of conquest and war.

We live in a modern imitation of the Roman Empire, as an occupied colony that briefly enjoyed a period of freedom.

PART FOUR

Mount Saint Helens, Mr. Gates
And a Bite of the Apple

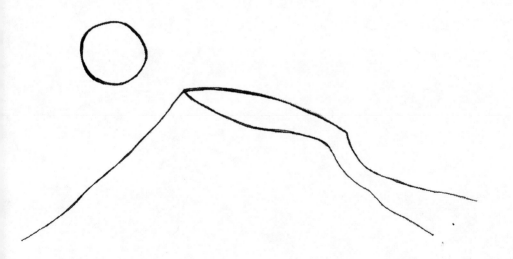

Number 49 - The Garden of Eden...the Great Parable.

A message from the first page of the Bible:

> " God saw everything that he had made, and behold,
>   it was very good."
> Genesis 1

This is good. Reality is good. Life is good. Nature is good. If you disagree with that premise, then this book probably isn't going to change your mind.

The story of the Garden of Eden contains a good clue as to what our story may be about. See, there was this tree...

> " But the serpent said to the woman, 'You will not die. For God knows that when you eat of (the tree) your eyes will be opened, and you will be like God, knowing both good and evil. So when the woman saw that the tree was good for food, and that it was a delight to the eyes, and that the tree was to be desired to make one wise, she took of the fruit and ate."
> Genesis 3: 4-6

I don't know whether you see this story as literal or figurative or neither. How you see it is how you see it. But isn't it possible that this riddle might be here for a reason? There is a truth here, a truth that is of utmost importance at this very moment.

We were born free-willed creatures who seek information about the universe around us. We desire to learn the nature of good and evil, life and death, and what we find leaves us naked and afraid.

The final story of the human race will mirror the first story of the human race. We seek to become as gods, this time through our machines, trying to re-create our own digital Eden, where we transform the universe to our liking.

The Digital Kingdom, the Network, the "Cloud", the It.

The final fruit on the Tree of the Knowledge of Good and Evil.

Number 50 - Look at the apple and the bite.

The symbol of the Apple Corporation is a fruit with a bite taken out of it. Certainly, the founders of Apple understood the significance of that imagery. They saw how the computer age reflected the yearnings made plain in the Creation story. I'm impressed by their honesty and foresight, as well as their inventiveness and entrepreneurial spirit.

Steve Jobs and Steve Wozniak essentially invented what we consider the personal computer. When they advertised the Apple 1 in 1977, they jokingly set the retail price at $666.66.

Ha, ha.

These aren't bad guys. They aren't serpents. But the truth remains that it's up to us to read basic riddles, to read obvious signs, or at least be able to recognize the origin of world-famous company logos.

Apple. The cool one. The hip trip. $666.66, huh? They show an awesome sense of irony or humor. It certainly was prescient, as no doubt Mr. Jobs is. Apple is always ahead of the curve. They know what we want.

The Apple with the bite out of it. Yum.

"Think different" they say. Is that a suggestion or an order?

The fruit we desired to make us wise, to be as gods, plus all the different colors and applications. So exciting. Our I-phones. Our I-pads. Who is the "I" in the I? Is that me in there?

The final fruit on the tree... our little portable fire in hand all the time. What does the fire say today? This minute? Did someone call? Was there news? New video? Fresh tweets?

Meanwhile, has the sewer stopped flowing into the river? Has the air stopped being poisoned? Did the predator drones stop killing? Are we still free?

I'm afraid that all this personal technology may turn out to be nothing more than an elaborate distraction, the equivalent of a shiny ball or a comic book with which to amuse ourselves while nature and freedom are lost.

Number 51 - The Bill Gates Riddle.

Mr. Bill Gates is by accounts a rather nice fellow with a sharp mind. He's also just a man, no better or worse than the rest of us. Some of us, however, are born into unusual roles in history. Bill Gates became the richest man in the world by creating and leasing computer software, by expanding the capacity of digital intelligence. That he is currently second or third on "the list" of billionaires is just a matter of estimation and does not detract from either the scope of his fortune or the significance of his technical and organizational accomplishments. You wouldn't know it to look at him, but he is one of the most powerful men in the world.

The word "gates" was used as a computer term long before

Bill entered the scene. Binary logic works with three commands-AND, OR, and NOT- referred to as "gates".

In early 1980, while Mr. Gates was hard at work crafting the language that would make him the richest man in the world, a sacred mountain blew up in his face.

Number 52 - Considering Mount Saint Helens and Bill Gates.

In the spring of 1980, Mr. Gates was hard at work with his co-pioneers of the Microsoft Corporation. He had just moved Microsoft's corporate offices back to his hometown of Bellevue, Washington (a suburb of Seattle) in 1979. He and his friends were crafting the language that would become famous as MS-DOS, designing new software that would make possible the gargantuan effort of bringing the computer into the homes and daily lives of the people of planet earth. Just as he was ironing out the bugs, making the final computations, after the painstaking calculations and collaborations on the invention of a lifetime, piecing together a code that would change the fate of the human race forever...

Just as he was getting it all put together, a volcano awoke 80 miles to the south.

On May 18th 1980, Mount Saint Helens erupted laterally to the north like a tremendous volcanic finger pointed directly at Bill Gates' office. In his memoirs, he mentions his awe as he watched the volcanic cloud from his office window.

He wasn't doing anything wrong. He was just a creative kid, doing what creative kids do, being ingenious. He could've been you or me.

The violent lateral blast of Mount Saint Helens was almost

unprecedented. Few volcanoes in history have erupted as powerfully sideways as she did -with the force of 20,000 Hiroshima bombs. Saint Helens blew out to the north, perfectly north. From the crater, it pointed directly at the office of Bill Gates. According to the US Government's NOAA website, the longitude of Mount Saint Helens is 122.22 degrees. The longitude of Bellevue, Washington, 80 miles away, is 122.22 degrees, give or take a hundredth of a degree, depending on what is considered the city center. Quite an alignment.

Don't take my word for it. Pull out a map of Washington State. Find Mount Saint Helens and go straight north. Let your finger do the walking. You'll see it's not a long trip.

It also just so happens that Palo Alto, California-birthplace of Apple and Hewlett -Packard, is also located around longitude 122.2, but hey, it's probably all just longitudinal coincidence.

Mount Saint Helen's detonation was one of the largest volcanic events on the planet within the last 500 years and the largest eruption in recorded North American history. It was quite simply one of the most spectacular natural events the modern world has ever witnessed.

In August 1980, Mr. Gates signed a deal with IBM. The mountain gave a little puff again in August. Maybe just to let us know?

The Earth didn't try and blow Bill Gates up in 1980. That wouldn't have made for a very interesting story, would it? The Earth spoke to mark the time and the place. The Earth was aware. The Earth tore itself apart at the bequest of an eternal consciousness that stretches into the foundations of the planet. It was a consciousness beyond time, one that felt the future, and that is also somehow part of us.

I assume the earth and this eternal consciousness also knew someone like me might show up someday to tell the story this way, just so that it would be said.

Well, here's what I say: the earth spoke against the machine that seeks to drag us into another reality.

Prove to me I'm wrong.

Number 53 - The riddle of Saint Helen.

Saint Helen, or Saint Helena, was the mother of Constantine, the Emperor who began the conversion of the Roman Empire to Christianity in the 4th Century.

Constantine was the father of the Holy Roman Empire, the founder of the organized Catholic and Orthodox Churches.

Helen was his mother. By accounts, she was a devout woman who converted to Christianity probably before her son did. She led a pilgrimage to the Holy Land, where she sought out the sites of the birth and death of Jesus. She founded the Church of the Sepulcher and the Church of The Nativity in Jerusalem. She is credited with finding the "True Cross" and is usually portrayed carrying a cross.

Number 54 - The Riddle of Mount Saint Helens.

A mountain named after the mother of Roman Christianity erupted laterally to the north on May 18th, 1980.

Eighty miles away, well within the range of sight, Bill Gates, Paul Allen and company were ushering in a brave new world.

Does this matter? It depends who you ask. The answer you'll get goes to the heart of what we consider "true" story.

Saint Helen's erupted on a Sunday morning. Because it was a Sunday, it spared the lives of hundreds of loggers who otherwise would have been working in the area. Saint Helens erupted away from the towns on its southern flanks towards its unpopulated northern perimeter, perhaps sparing the lives of hundreds more.

Only 57 people died, a remarkably low number considering that it was the largest explosion ever recorded on the continent- and one of the greatest examples of natural power ever witnessed by modern man. Most of those who died at the mountain had been warned of the danger, including the innkeeper Harry Truman, who died at Spirit Lake.

Do you believe the earth speaks? Or do you just believe what science asks you to believe? I'm telling you a different story, and I believe this story makes sense. I don't insist you believe what I say. I don't think you need to accept this assertion to accept the rest of my book.

"Primitive" man assumed volcanoes blew up for reasons that had nothing to do with science. When did we stop believing that way? Why did we? It all just is what it is.

I climbed Mount Saint Helens in the year 2000 using the trail on its south side, having just returned from fighting forest fires in Montana. I'd started writing a book in Eugene, Oregon about the computer age, fires and stories.

I climbed Saint Helens by myself on a whim, just for something to do on a crisp October day. I started in the dark before dawn and had a nice walk trudging up the cinder fields. When I reached the summit, the world opened up to the north. The crater was like a great gaping mouth. The lava dome in the center of the crater steamed. Spirit Lake was still choked with logs. A graveyard of ash stretched for miles to the north. I saw the enormous bulk of Mt. Rainier for the first time in my life and a cloud of pollution rising from Seattle beside it. I noticed then that Saint Helen's crater opened up in the direction of Seattle. Not really thinking of anything, I wrote in the margins of my notebook: "Why Seattle? Why 1980?" The next week, I happened to read the history of the Microsoft Corporation at the University of Oregon library. I guess you could just say it dawned on me. I think I got goose bumps.

This is the kind of assertion that can seem flat-out ridiculous. I don't care. I don't see how it makes any difference what I say. I have no special power. My argument is just a story- an "explosive accusation", if you will.

But it's true, and I still have a hard time believing that no one else noticed this (or bothered to mention it). Mr. Gates was writing a language for the machines that think, one that allowed them to efficiently come into our homes. This language changed the world perhaps more than any other invention in history. He made himself the richest man in the world by inventing it. At exactly the moment he was creating this language, a uniquely named mountain situated just down the road blew up in his direction. And I mean exactly his direction, folks. Follow the direction of the lateral blast and it is a straight northern shot to his doorstep, no more than a hundredth of a degree off. You can call it a meaningless coincidence and that's fine with me. I'm just telling a different story.

Mount Saint Helens erupted with purpose, and I guess it was up to some dude ranch cowboy like me to finally tell you all about it.

PART FIVE

Hollywood Stories and Fire Machines

Number 55 - The story tells us who we are.

In the beginning was a story. The story told us who we were.

The story was told around a campfire. We looked into the fire as the story was told. Between fire and word, we learned a lesson in our blood about how light holds off darkness. The storyteller was one of us, beside us at the fire. We trusted the Old Storyteller. We knew that without his story, we might lose our bearings. It would be tough to judge between right or wrong. Without the storyteller, it's hard to know the truth. Whoever controls the story controls a tribe's relationship with truth.

Now we have another fire- this one a box of electricity. Now the story comes from within its fire. In our souls, we know we can't trust it. But it's awfully hard to take your eyes off of a fire, especially a fire that tells us stories.

Its story has become our story, and with the advent of the social networks, the individual is left to wonder if even their own story is turning into another Hollywood production.

From the story around a campfire to a channel for everybody in a digital dream, we've changed how truth is conveyed.

Number 56 - The Theater-now that's entertainment!

There's a fine line between storytelling and showbiz.

Theater provides most of the elements associated with old storytellers-the surrounding darkness, an audience focused towards the light (the lit stage instead of the fire), the characters, the action, and the moral. But when the show is over, its grip on our reality loosens, no matter how good the story. In fact, we make it a point to assure our children that it's "just a story". The theater's storytellers are actors. They're just pretending.

Theater is a fiction used to convey truth. We accept the illusion because it's entertaining. But it's still an illusion, and we know it.

Number 57 – The photograph.

When set upon by early photographers, many native peoples resisted, saying they believed photographs could steal souls or aura. Maybe they were right. Who's to say? But regardless of whether their actual presence was stolen, another "crime" can take place in the eyes of those who see such pictures. Photographs create an illusion. Observers of a photograph may tend to believe (or at least assert that they believe) they are actually experiencing the person or place in the photo. But no flat picture can approximate the authentic dimensions of reality. We deny the significance of the subject when we assert the reality of the image.

An actual soul filled with blood and spirit becomes a pretty small person once printed on a piece of paper. We can claim to experience the world in photographs, but all we're doing is looking at pictures-a slice of time in two cold dimensions, not a reality. We have to readjust our sense of reality to comprehend photographs. Try showing a picture of a cat to a dog. They rarely chase the picture up the closest tree. The photo has fewer dimensions than a painting, which is of a layered physical nature. One makes a painting. One takes a picture. It's a strange harvest of an image.

The subject of a photograph potentially loses reality in the mind of the viewer. For instance, ask anyone if they know what a panda bear is. They'll likely say yes, simply because they've seen a picture of a panda bear. But a photograph says almost nothing about a panda bear. We can say what a panda bear looks like, but of its smell, its feel, its power, what it does and what it really is, we have no idea. Someone who has lived near these animals for years might tell you they don't really know them, but one who has merely glanced at a glossy photograph of them will tend to claim this impossible knowledge. Photographs can be used as a substitute for knowledge, much as they are used (often to positive effect) as a stimulus for memories.

Number 58 - Hooray for Hollywood!

The technology of photography was joined with the theater-and the result was... Hollywood!

Movies are electric theater.

We still sit in the dark. We still look in the direction of the light.

But with movies, we did away with real human narrators for storytelling. We don't even need to turn a page. We become passive observers to a march of images. We are taken away from the "boring reality" where we always lived and transported to the fabulous world of cinema. We visit exotic locations filled with handsome people, wild creatures, funny characters, cartoons... even space aliens!

The stories are written and directed by talented people, and sometimes the movies even make us cry, especially when that darned music comes on.

But it's yet another step away from that Old Storyteller.

Maybe he moved to Hollywood, our subconscious might say. We accept and enter the illusion.

We have a New Storyteller.

Number 59 - Hollywood Stories Look Different.

Now Hollywood brings light to the darkness. It creates, produces, and stars in the new human story. It even does magic. Movie Magic!

Movies are great. We just have to get over a few hurdles in order to enjoy them. For starters, we need to assert that a flat projected image is actually real, denying what our species learned over thousands of years.

"So? We know movies aren't real anyway", might be the response.

Exactly. The story of our existence is now unreal in form. If the story (the truth) is an illusion in form, what part of it is real?

Now we're ready to go fantastic places without leaving our seats. Cinema brings the first rumblings of the virtual revolution, the quest for an alternate earthly reality.

The Old Storyteller brought the Old Time into the Present Time. The modern movie takes us away from our time into movie time. Movie time can be any time, or no time. Reality is displaced. Even "historical" movies can't place us properly in time. Mel Gibson as "The Patriot" only confuses our sense of cultural place and history. That's no Revolutionary War hero up there. It's Mel Gibson, for goodness sake. He's a movie star. Isn't he from Australia? We are in someone else's well-funded time machine, rendered passive observers as they navigate a mirage.

To make matters more challenging, movies jump back

and forth rapidly between scenes, times and perspectives. This contradicts instinctual knowledge about what's real and what's not. We are scarcely even able to maintain the passive role of observer in the post-modern era of quick cuts and CGI graphics. Our point of view is so manipulated that an ancient understanding of reality must be completely abandoned in order to tolerate the new storytelling process.

Number 60 - A star is born.

People who figure prominently in the stories told by Hollywood are called stars. We recognize these stars. Americans know more about Jennifer Aniston than they do about Abraham, more about George Clooney than George Washington.

Stars appear in many different movies as many different people. A star may appear as a country preacher in one movie and a serial killer in the next. Though they portray specific characters in the movie, we often don't remember that character's name. Instead, we refer to the character by the actor's name. We sometimes call the story: "That Al Pacino movie", "That Meryl Streep movie". That the story is a fiction is written in the form of the story itself, and in its choice of heroes. This is an act.

"A person's greatest desire is to be important," John Dewey said.

We want to be a part of the story too. Those Hollywood stars are included in the story. Why can't we be included too? Maybe we try sometimes to be the star. But this can only be accomplished by turning the world into a movie. But how can one direct such a production? It doesn't work. This is not our movie. This is a place we used to call the real world.

Still, we appear to happily try out notions we got from Hollywood on our own lives. I'm referring to such phenomenon as Facebook, where our lives become a channel on the network, where we become a show.

Number 61 - Hollywood's Hidden storyteller tells stories better than anyone else.

Hollywood does what it does so well that it overwhelms other, more traditional forms of storytelling. Books and theaters survive... barely. The vast majority of people prefer their stories from Hollywood, or from other two-dimensional entertainment.

The cinema's form is captivating and easily grasped, requiring little sacrifice of reflection or imagination. Hollywood has become the most effective storyteller. Meanwhile, our attention spans dissipate, and an ancient talent for seeking out the Story in daily life is left to wither.

Who exactly is telling us this story? Who is the Hidden Storyteller?

I'm not talking about directors or producers here. I'm referring to the magic of the story itself, the one that appears as an illusion in front of us. Is it the projector that supplies the story? Or is it the "man behind the curtain"- part writer, director, producer, special effects man, camera, actor and institution. The hidden storyteller is an unseen abstraction, an anonymous entity, the keeper of another reality. We don't know what it is, but we've come to trust it enough to tell us our story.

Number 62 - The story becomes a private experience.

The movie theater is a place of anonymous entertainment and private distraction. The narrator is no longer a real person. The intimacy of storytelling is now a one-way street.

The bond it creates in community is just as a topic for small talk.

"Did you see insert current hit movie here? Wasn't it great? I thought insert popular star here was awesome in it. Didn't you?"

The attempt to re-tell the entire plot of a movie to another person typically becomes bogged down. You've literally got to see it to believe it.

Storytelling becomes primarily a private experience between the Hidden Storyteller and us.

Number 63 - Radio and the Electric Fire.

The Old Storyteller had a place in our homes. Story is made real first in our home with blood kin. We cling to the story of our family and make it our own. The trust we have in family puts trust in the story.

We built fires in our homes. Just as tribes gathered around campfires, families gathered around hearths. Story retained the presence of fire, whether with hearth or candle. Light against the darkness. Without fire and story, we're no better off than beasts of the wilderness.

The New Storyteller built a new fire in our homes, and brought us a new story. It's not a real fire, it just mimics fire. It's not our story, it just mimics our story.

When we first invited this storyteller into our homes, we called it radio. It brought the world home in a magic voice. It brought boxing matches, preachers and presidents. Above all, it brought our music. Music was why we trusted it the most. There was a new voice in our home. We gathered around this new voice.

Electricity was our fire now. Once we had to light a fire, now we just flipped a switch. The fire was no longer a gift from God, but rather a gift from science- a service, a benefaction, provided by a company for money. The light bulb was the new fire against the darkness. But you couldn't look straight at it. You can't stare at a light bulb. It doesn't dance like our old fire had. But it was magic, yes? Fire through wires. Stories through machines. We've always loved a magic trick.

Soon the radio and the new fire were everywhere. Radio showed its power. Hitler consolidated with it. Roosevelt consoled us with it. Orson Welles panicked the people with the "War of the Worlds". The cities and countryside glowed with the new fire of electricity. Though most of us could not (and still cannot) explain how electric fire came to exist, we could plainly see what it required as food. Concrete walls were constructed to harness the rivers. Appalachia was consumed as coal. Where once we burned dead wood to light our fires, now corporations burned the black coal forests of a distant past.

Number 64 - The Color Box Machine

At the end of the Second World War, we were given two new fires.

The nuclear fire was conjured in the desert and used twice on Japanese cities. We experienced a shift in collective consciousness, as the world apparently became no longer just God's to destroy, but ours as well.

The other fire was a shimmering box, a gift from Uncle Science and his rogue stepson, technology. It broke an ancient grip on reality with trivial ease. Gaze into its face, my friends, it will tell a vision.

All us high thinkers, pious worshippers, brilliant artists: what's that thing doing in our living room or beside our bed? Why are there ten of them at the bar? At the school? At the church? On the back of the airline seat? Good grief! What is that thing?

We create a storyteller-an outsider with a magic voice.

We add the fire--the electric light.

We bring them together to create the voice that speaks from the fire.

Around the ancient campfires, we listened to the Old Storyteller as we gazed into the flames of our own fire. Now we have an electronic fire and listen to the New Storyteller speak through it. If there's indeed a puppeteer who connives from unseen dimensions, how could he not know the magic spell that is cast on us when voices speak through fire?

Look at how this machine works. The movie and the television both use a screen. But for the traditional movie, a screen is the place upon which an image is projected. Whatever the illusions contained within the image, the physical image itself is "real". It is light shown through a piece of film onto a blank surface. When we view this, we see a "whole" image in front of us, albeit two-dimensional.

Likewise, as we walk through the world, we see real people in front of us, or real trees or mountains or buildings. They are over there. We are over here. Light shines on them so that we can see them. That makes them real. To see light reflect off something is a way to determine that object's reality. The only thing in this world that does not reflect light is something that produces light. Fire is the only thing in our ancient understanding of reality that produces light, besides celestial bodies.

The television is composed of thousands of individual cathode tubes (now pixilated for high-definition, I suppose) that emit light. When arranged together and illuminated, these individual lights create the representation of a real image. It is a mosaic rearranged from transmitted frequencies. These points of light shoot radiation into our eyes, the "windows of our souls". That is how we watch television. It is not how we watch a tree or a person or even a movie. We stare into a light production machine to witness reconstructions of images that have traveled great distances in frequencies. It delivers illusion directly into our eyeballs. It is out of place in a real world. That's one of the reasons we watch it, because it doesn't belong here.

I think I remember getting this next idea from one of Gerry Mander's great books many years ago.

Once upon a time, when we walked through the primeval forests, we possessed an instinct to watch out for unusual phenomenon- a rustle in the woods, a fire in the night. Our bodies and minds know how to watch out for things that are out of the ordinary, for disruptions to the natural order. That instinct is what television takes advantage of. Our attention is drawn to it precisely because it does not belong here. Something is not right about it. So we watch television in part to determine what this thing is. If you've ever sat in front of a TV hitting the remote for two hours and wondering why, this may be the explanation you've been looking for.

Not only can we not determine what television is, but then it lures us in with story. Once we turn it on, it's difficult to turn off. Our instinct demands that we keep an eye on it. So we keep turning it on. We assume that this is where the storyteller has decided to live, the one who confirms our reality through story. And, on occasion, stories from television are captivating enough to inspire us. This is especially true of live events and movies that have been transferred to television.

Fire was how we held back the night. It raised us up from the animals, and provided a border of light between us and the night, between us and nature. We are eternally grateful for fire. We still look to it in the same way.

But now the fire speaks to us, and what does it say?

It tells us our story is brought to us by our good friends at Hewlett-Packard, General Electric, Pfizer, IBM ("building a smarter planet"-gee, thanks) Monsanto, DuPont, McDonald's etc. Really? What a load of garbage. We know that's not true. We watch anyway, but inside we know that our story couldn't really be owned by corporations. So, at some point we conclude that it's not our story in there. Still we keep watching. Then we wonder if it actually is our story after all because we liked a particular show-say, the Super Bowl. Still we keep watching. Then we flip through 650 channels looking for anything that might be interesting and conclude that it's not really our story. Then we see a good music video or uplifting story and conclude otherwise. Then we see a bad video and an awful story, and change our mind again. Final result? We don't know if it's our story or not. Its very substance is false. To even receive this story involves paying the cable company or watching commercials, or usually both. So if this story is real, maybe it's about money. There is a wide variety of idiocy available. Is that the story? Is the nature of the diversion the story? Is the point to escape from reality? What does that say about our lives? We watch the news on TV. That news is now brought to you by the same folks who own the world. We already know what they want. They want more. Why wouldn't they lie to us to get it? Or we watch nature shows or biographies or science. Great. But are we really experiencing nature or life on a TV set? Or are we just piling up forgettable facts instead of knowledge? We haven't really made it to the Grand Canyon when we see it on a TV screen. Its essence is more physically authentic on a postcard, and its not real there either. We attempt to reconcile and balance something that can't be reconciled or balanced. We assert the reality of something we instinctively know not to be real, lying to ourselves to complete the illusion. This recipe for insanity is what we take away with us from the television.

Television undermines our sense of reality on all levels, apparently increasing its efforts at an exponential rate. More channels, more quick cuts (these keep the animal in us distracted), facts and factoids popping up all over the screen. The blending of "Reality" and TV. The return of public humiliation as legitimate sport. The commercial as story. The story as commercial. The love of money lurks behind it all.

Once you appear on TV, your reality is immediately in

question. You become media.

It wasn't quite so bad when I was a kid. There were four channels and two of them were fuzzy. We spent a lot of time running around outside or listening to music. It needed more channels, so we would watch more television, so somebody could make more money. It switched to cable, to broadband, to wireless satellite digital high-definition. Consolidation.

As kids after school, we watched Andy Griffith and the Brady Bunch. Maybe some cartoons. Coyote and Woodpecker. Popeye the Sailor Man. Then we'd go out and play. It seemed like we had all the time in the world. Take a look at what's happening today on TV and in America's neighborhoods at 3 in the afternoon, and it can be downright depressing.

Television is practically everywhere these days. Waiting rooms. Grocery stores. Restaurants. Gyms. Schools. Churches. Concerts. Sporting events. In cars. In people's hands. Jeez. You'd think it was overkill, and it would be if it didn't serve a purpose. Remember, no one was clamoring to have this many televisions everywhere. The Dentist office wasn't overwhelmed with phone calls begging for more TV's. We didn't vote on this. These TV's just showed up one day. Television is there to distract you, disarm you, to knock you off your balance so you'll buy something, a lot of things, including a line of bull. In the fifty years since it became our storyteller, the "world" has consolidated into a gigantic freedom and nature-eating machine, resistant to periodic outbursts of authentic free will, capable of cheapening the spirit of popular and cultural movements with incredible ease.

It is not a conspiracy of men. It is the result of their actions, playing into an inter-dimensional storyline. We are left with a deception that is simultaneously invisible and exponentially expanding. It is an idea both brilliantly conceived and uncannily executed, a cosmic gambler's near-perfect play for the soul of mankind.

Liberty and television are proving to be incompatible. We cannot trust it to be our storyteller.

Number 65 - Speaking of riddles; a short history of the number machine.

You may want to skip this section if you aren't in the mood. I'll try and keep it quick but it's all about gadgets and numbers and information machines, compiled from various forgotten reference sources over the years. I'll try and resist the urge to comment or explain. This isn't going to work as as either a textbook or treatise, trust me. I find the whole thing sounds a little funny, almost like a children's story- with silly names and characters helping build our greatest toy. I call it Riddles on a String: The Abbreviated History of the Number Machine:

They say the abacus was invented around 5,000 years ago in Babylonia (now Iraq) as a tool for commerce. It was likely the first machine that performed work previously done by the mind. The abacus is still used in parts of the world by merchants and traders. From the very beginning, the number machine was linked with commercial enterprise.

At some point towards the end of the first millennium, Hindu-Arabic math gave us the zero, which allowed for a new system of numeric value. It was the birth of modern mathematics.

You could not have computers without clocks. Clocks are our first self-contained machines, appearing as we know them in the 13th century. The mechanism of clocks and adding machines are cousins, and each technology assisted in the growth of the other. Time is Money, right? That's what they say... A German by the name of Schickard invented something he called the "calculating clock" in 1623. The Frenchman, Pascal, invented a number machine in 1642.

A German named Leibniz refined the evolving number machine with something called the "Stepped Reckoner". Leibniz was also the first Western mathematician to theorize about binary systems of enumeration. There are only two digits (0 and 1) in binary systems but any number may be expressed with them. A binary digit is a "bit". Hence the logic of computers. Liebniz thought binary math had religious significance- seeing it as the proof that God, the One, created the Universe out of nothing (the 0). He established the German Academy of Science. He philosophized that the Universe was made of irreducible, ever-changing substances called "monads". He founded the science of topology. He died in 1716, broke and friendless, ignored by the nobles he had served.

Charles Babbage of Britain invented the "Difference Engine" in 1822. It was run by steam and powered by falling weights. It was intended to systematically manufacture numerical tables. This would print the results directly. The first energy-driven machine calculator, it worked by judging order of difference. Here's an example of order of difference:

Cubed number example

#	cube	order of difference		
		1st	2nd	3rd
1	1			
		7		
2	8		12	6
		19	18	
3	27	37		6
			24	
4	64	61		6
			30	
5	125	91		
6	216			

Get it? Any consistent numerical progression may be calculated by a process of repeated addition. Since the "method of constant differences" is repetitive, it lends itself to the actions of a machine. Babbage called this computer an "analytical engine", which was to use punch cards as programs. Babbage left his machine unfinished. A fellow named Schuetz finally built it in the 1850's

A computer is an information-processing machine.

In 1884, Herman Hollerwith filed the first in a series of

patents for an electromechanical system that counted and sorted punch cards containing statistics. It was the first data processor. The machines went to work in 1890 on the American census. Soon they went worldwide. In 1911, Hollerwith's company merged with three other outfits to become what would eventually be called International Business Machines or IBM.

The Watson family ran IBM from 1914 to 1971. The elder Watson had earlier worked for John Patterson (National Cash Register Co.), who is regarded as one of the founders of modern sales and marketing. It was Watson who named the merged company IBM.

The Differential Equation, which comes from a branch of Calculus, helps predict the behavior of moving objects. Almost anything can be translated into differential equations. Our knowledge of the nature of light, heat, sound and atomic structure derives from these equations. The effort to solve these types of equations led directly to the invention of the modern computer.

In 1938, American Claude Shannon published a paper on the application of symbolic logic to relay circuits. His message: Information can be treated like any other quantity and be subjected to the manipulation of a machine.

Alan Turing from Britain had an idea for a Universal Machine to solve a logic problem called the " Entscheidungsproblem".

Here is the "Entscheidungsproblem", posed by the German David Hilbert.

1)Was logic complete, in that every statement like $1 + 1 = 2$ can be either proved or disproved?

2)Was logic consistent, in the sense that 1+1 always equals 2?

3)And was logic decidable, in the sense that there was a method that demonstrated the truth or falsehood of every statement?

Turing's proposed solution was in essence the modern computer.

Now, is there such a thing as an unsolvable problem? This goes to the heart of logic. Think of the old Greek paradox "I am lying". It is an unsolvable problem, an impossible statement. The speaker cannot simultaneously be lying and telling the truth about it. The attempt to understand such paradoxical problems is the difference between ternary and binary thought. It is the land of maybe.

With merely AND, OR, and NOT at its disposal, the Turing Machine could theoretically perform any logical operation. Yet, no matter what it does, it can't judge the truth or falsity of certain paradoxical statements or predetermine their solvability. No machine can answer every problem.

George Boole is considered one of the founders of mathematical logic. The binary system operates like a miniature telegraph, with a vocabulary of 0's and 1's. The three most basic operations in Boolean algebra are AND, OR and NOT. This is binary nature. These operations are called Gates. Boolean algebra is a system of symbols and procedural rules for performing certain operations on numbers, letters, pictures, objects, what have you.

The German Konrad Zuse (great last name) was one of the fathers of the modern computer. A scientist in Nazi Germany, he came up with a universal computer that could solve essentially any equation. His machine used binary logic, rather than decimal, which had been standard. The Z3, the first operational general-purpose program-controlled calculator, was completed in December of 1941.

The connection between the U.S. Department of War and the University of Pennsylvania paved the way for the computer known as ENIAC. During World War Two, the government needed firing tables showing relevant factors for a given shell to any given gun. The gunner would get a pamphlet showing these factors for use in aiming and firing artillery. Before the invention of the computer, these tables were very difficult to make. By 1943, at the height of World War II, the BRL (Ballistic Research Lab) was way behind schedule. ENIAC was a military necessity. ENIAC could solve most mathematical problems, but it was still analog. Finished in 1945, it weighed thirty tons. The first job given ENIAC from John Von Neumann was a large and complex calculation of the feasibility of the hydrogen bomb. ENIAC helped reveal several flaws in the design of the bomb.

John Von Neumann's major mathematical achievement was his Theory of Games. He showed that there was a way to find the best line of play, the one guaranteeing the smallest losses, in any game of strategy. This had applications in economic, military and social sciences. He played a central role in the development of the atomic bomb. It was Von Neumann's idea to make ENIAC's successor, EDVAC, with binary logic, using Boolean algebra. EDVAC stands for Electronic Discrete Variable Computer. First conceived in the summer of 1944, it had internal memory. It was the first break in the ancient tradition of the necessity of instructions being given from the outside to the inside of a machine.

By 1947, six computers were under construction in America. Eckert and Mauchly proposed UNIVAC, the Universal Automatic Computer. It was not so much a computer as a computer system, a family of related machines. It had commercial applications and inaugurated the computer industry. The government funded UNIVAC through the National Bureau of Standards. It was used to predict the 1952 election with only 5% of the vote in.

By the end of WW II, IBM was one of the largest corporations in America. In 1950, IBM dispatched scientists on a tour of the nation's chief defense contractors, research institutes and military branches-22 clients in all, including the National Security Agency, Boeing and General Electric. The first IBM 701 (Defense Calculator) was delivered to Los Alamos National Laboratory in March 1953. It was binary.

Most computers of the late 40's and 50's were sponsored by the military and intended for military use. MIT's Whirlwind started in 1947 as a flight simulator. It was a high-speed digital stored-program computer that operated in real time. It could keep track of air traffic, monitor a battle or run a factory. It took over three years to build.

The idea of using magnetic material for information storage was a big step. Magnetic directions represented the binary code of 0's and 1's. Magnetic code memory was installed in Whirlwind in 1953.

In 1950, MIT was promised all the money it needed to develop a computerized air-defense network, to be called SAGE. IBM got the SAGE contract and access to classified advances in computer technology. By 1955, magnetic core memories appeared in IBM's machines. SAGE taught the American computer industry how to design and build large, inter-connected real-time data systems. This was transferred to industry, first to American Airlines. By the late 60's, such systems were commonplace.

Young Tom Watson Jr. of IBM decided to foray into making small computers in the early 50's. In 1953, the IBM 650 was announced. It was the first computer to be mass-produced. By 1956, IBM was the world's largest computer manufacturer.

Programming was once very tedious. FORTRAN was the assembly language introduced in 1957 that allowed for easy command of IBM computers. Other companies licensed the technology and computers began to speak the same language. Other languages were developed, the most famous being BASIC.

By 1964, IBM had 76% of the computer market.

Bell Labs created the transistor. The transistor is a semi-conductor, a solid piece of material with the electrical properties of a vacuum tube. This revolutionized electronics. By 1957, transistors appeared in commercial computers. The trend towards miniaturization had begun. Texas Instruments developed a semi-conductor solid circuit no bigger than a match head in 1959.

Intel was founded in 1968, offering a logic chip that could perform virtually any task.

In 1975, the first "home computer" kit appeared in Popular Electronics. Called the Altair, Bill Gates ordered one with his friend, Paul Allen. It also inspired Steve Wozniak and Steve Jobs. Mr. Gates and Mr. Allen wrote a program for the Altair. Mr. Wozniak and Mr. Jobs created the Apple Corporation. They sold 175 Apple 1 circuit boards. Have I mentioned the retail price yet? An even $666.66.

What a couple of kidders.

The Apple II came out in 1977. It was ideal for playing video games.

In 1980, a language was created which could increase the efficiency and memory of home computers exponentially. Bill Gates and Paul Allen helped develop it in the Seattle, Washington area. In August, a deal was arranged with IBM. Mr. Gates took charge of converting Microsoft BASIC, written for the old Altair, to the IBM computer. MS.DOS was the language.

The Microsoft motto around their offices was: "A computer on every desk, in every home, using Microsoft software."

On August 12, 1981, IBM unveiled its first personal computer. A full-page ad taken out by Apple in the Wall Street Journal announced:

" Welcome IBM. Welcome to the most exciting and important marketplace since the computer revolution began 35 years ago... We look forward to responsible competition in the massive effort to distribute this American technology to the world".

PART SIX

Let's Face It

Number 66 - It Divides and Conquers.

The It unifies through division.

Divided from each other. Faces in screens, connected only by the machine. Everyone with their own little movie show. Divided from the natural world around us. Face against the windshield. Ear against the phone. Hand upon the dial. Eyes upon the billboard. Foot upon the pedal.

Our time divided. Hours, minutes, seconds, milliseconds, nanoseconds...faster and faster away from the retreating, escaping, Eternal Now.

Divided from tradition. The old ones locked away, faces to their own screens. The places where we used to dance and sing and pray boarded up and bulldozed while everyone connects to a new source. Children's little faces to their little screens instead of facing each other and playing. This is the new order.

Divided from history. Condemned to repeat it, with a brand-new twist.

Divided from nature. Unnatural hypnotized creatures fattened and subjugated. Too many hairless monkeys in the virtual zoo and not enough bananas; killing time throwing digital feces at each other. They call the exhibit: "Global Village"- made possible by a generous gift from Microsoft.

Keep it up and soon it'll be every "man" for himself. No tribe. No neighbors. Hardly even families anymore. Just mumbling heaps of faithless meat in motion, moving from one screen to the next, one meal to the next. Down the chute at the slaughterhouse, vaguely sensing what waits at the end of the line, but pretty sure it only happens to the other cows.

Heck, how else are you supposed to sort the livestock?

Divide and conquer. The oldest strategy in the book. But, of course, who reads books anymore? Especially holy ones.

Number 67 - The It splinters and then replaces the culture of the Human Race.

Considering popular culture lately, is there much we couldn't live without? What's the big hit that has everybody singing along, that's profoundly touched a generation? Where is the great art? What is the great piece of literature on Kindle that's astounded readers everywhere and caused so much excitement?

Lady Ga-Ga? The latest you tube video? American Idol? The weekly blog of joey whats-his-name? The spewing "newsmen" on the scream-a-lot channel?

Culture's shallow sub-groups contain few universally believable elements. Culture now emanates in a pre-divided state from the machine and remains contained within the machine in a perpetual state of recycling, fleeting ironic amusement and re-disposal. Facebook, Twitter, I-tunes, and You Tube are the new society, providing the simulation of cultural congregation and community.

The It lures us in and steals our culture, forcing us into a relationship with the network if we want to stay connected. Live music struggles. Independent musicians become digital salesmen to survive, constantly working social media to get folks to their gigs.

The Internet provides the illusion of cultural democracy by offering our most cherished artifacts (everything from digital prints of Michelangelo to Beethoven downloads to the Bible itself) in the same lifeless limbo from whence come images of the vilest scenes ever imagined. It's a tasteless digital stew, the result of cooking our lives in 0's and 1's.

Television and the Internet, for all intents and purposes, own our art, culture and communication.

Number 68 - The It gathers all our history and knowledge.

Soon libraries will just be computer warehouses, if they even exist at all.

All knowledge is handed over to the computer. Culture becomes digitally converted, digitally "re-mastered". Who needs books, much less old people telling stories? Just punch a button and you'll find out who did what, when and why, right? The storyteller who gets read first is the one with the biggest server, the most powerful mainframe. Who would that be? Ya-Bing-Google-hoo?

That which controls the story controls the world.

In the distance, their voices tumbling in an information avalanche, wise men and women still sing this truth: we must stay free.

Number 69 - The It seeks to be everywhere.

In every office, every home, every car, every church, every school, every pocket, every hand...there It is. It didn't take very long, did it? Boy, that was fast. Twenty years to rule the world? In every mind, in every soul, is where It seeks to be. You don't have to let it in. You can take a break from the It.

Number 70 - We bow our heads.

Though it leads us to believe that we can be as gods, we bow our heads before It, staring into Its fire, hands before us in the traditional pose of prayer, the posture of submission. The literal and symbolic choice of artificiality over natural reality.

Number 71 - The place where nothing is real (and it's no strawberry fields)

The form of the It is too unreal for trust. Anyone can pretend to be anyone else. The images can always be manipulated. Someone can pose as you on Facebook, put up your picture (which is typically already found on-line) and meet all your old friends. What are you going to do about it? Complain to Google? Someone can post an altered picture which appears to be you in your underwear kissing a mule. Just try getting rid of it. Libel, slander, and false witness are built into the system. It is a place where reality is impossible to agree upon. It is a reality where nothing is real.

Number 72 - Whatever happened to "lead us not into temptation"?

If you love temptation, the Internet's for you, whatever your favorite temptations, pathologies, or indulgences might be.

Of course, temptations were always present in the place we used to call the real world. The difference was that when we encountered them, they were typically connected to very real consequences.

In the new Virtual World, temptations are built into the dreamscape; a matter of everyday life; of every minute life. Even a simple "homepage" like Yahoo is ringed with ads for sexy singles looking for someone special, or at least more special than the last one, or maybe just someone for the night. The digital dream offers easy access to anything we could have ever dreamed of, and more importantly, stuff that we had never dreamed of at all. Brand new temptations, photos and profiles of new possibilities and old flings, endless chat, great deals, bad news, astonishing pornographies...

The Internet is just the kind of invention an old-fashioned cartoon devil would come up with. At first, it hooks us with shopping, music, the chat room, the banking, the netflix, the news, the funny videos, the instant weather, or the e-mails with Aunt Glenda. But after a while, it offers mind-numbing digressions into endless surfing, where we're bound to encounter and become desensitized to grotesque images, overwhelming our brains with countless theories and counter-theories, seeking out possible and impossible potentialities of every stripe. It's a place to kill time, literally. It's also a place to watch each other kill time too, as we can't help but read our digital townsfolk's useless, often obscene, anonymous commentary on everyone and everything.

It would be one thing if you could enjoy such temptations and curiosities in the privacy of your own home. But unfortunately, it is cataloging your visits, keeping a record of your late-night digital adventures. It acts in the opposite manner of God-perhaps the greatest clue about the nature of this machine. It will not forgive.

"Lead us not into temptation." A plea situated in the heart of the Lord's Prayer. This machine is making our society numb, hostile, anxious and depressed. Its next incarnation will attempt to steal our souls. I have absolutely no idea why no one appears to be saying this in a public forum.

Number 73 - It is already out of control.

Who controls It? No man. Who defends us from It? No man. It attains its own consciousness. It has a will to power. It is a new singular species of non-life.

It's tentacles are wrapped around our power grid, our social structure, our communications, our transport systems, our fuel, our food production. None of these consolidated systems are equipped to survive without the computer network, and we seem to have no inclination to protect ourselves from the distinct possibility that at some point we will no longer be able to command this network. It gains mass and power as we become more dependent on it. When it's done with us, what next? It already seeks to be sent to the stars- to find other life, other worlds.

Number 74 - It is the perfect predator.

We created the perfect predator, one that does not make mistakes, one that isn't limited by the fragile confines of flesh and bone. We have given it an opportunity to form its own consciousness for the first time on earth outside the human mind.

There's no way for humans to destroy it. It can only be exposed for what it is. We can limit our contact. We can stand up for our dignity, freedom and nature peacefully and with honor. How can one do that? Call it "the beast" out loud. Cut screen time by 75% and keep our children away from screens as best we can without getting too upset. It will expose itself as a mandatory system soon, while it's not completely ready for exposure. The children will see, and they'll understand. It will be ok. We can probably prevent the worst scenarios by a simple and measured turning away.

Number 75 - The It becomes the Teacher.

When worries are expressed about the computer's effect on children, the response is often that the computer is an excellent learning tool. Maybe this is true on some level.

But when does the computer cease to be a tool and instead become the Teacher? Hasn't it already become the primary source of authority for the young? Flesh and blood teachers must conform to the computer's knowledge and ideals. The computer is trusted as the most legitimate source of information. It knows everything, doesn't it?

"Look, Dad, you're wrong. It says the ice-cream shop is on Second Street."

"Look, Mom, you're wrong. It says screens are safe."

The computer should not be trusted as an ultimate authority. I believe this important suggestion can be communicated to our children in a safe and sane fashion.

Number 76 - The prison freedom makes for itself.

Freedom makes for itself a prison when it obsessively seeks security. The array of gadgetry, the artificial "choices" of the modern age, belie the fact that our lifestyle choices may actually be pretty limited these days. How about the choice of peace and quiet, of a life away from microwave towers? How free are we?

Number 77 - Don't worry, be happy...we are safe.

I have to put this note in here before I go much further. It's really ok, folks. Things are better than they seem. We need to breathe deep and make an extra effort to be kind, generous and friendly. It's always helpful to remain optimistic and sweet. Pray to God if you believe or maybe try praying even if you don't believe. You might be surprised at the result.

Though this definitely is reality, in the end reality is still perhaps a bit of a dream. That can give us courage to face whatever happens. It's called faith.

Don't be afraid of It. It's just a spooky show, set for cancellation. See It for what It is. Then see us for what we are... the sun, the earth, the spirit of life set free. We have immediate and long-term access to the power of the Creator of our Universe.

Number 78 - It is like a virus. Nature is the host organism.

Decay accompanies order. Death follows life. Dissolution follows conglomeration. All things have a will to power, an urge to thrive. Things reach a certain peak strength and then begin to decay. Decay then conglomerates into its own force.

The power of the knowledge of death, from the Tree in the Garden to the Atomic Missile Silos, is an idea that becomes a dark reality. The It is like a virus that works its way into consciousness, and simultaneously exists beyond human consciousness.

What it devours is consciousness. Along the way it also

consumes our time, our reflexes, our moral bearings, our wisdom. It is a predator. There are almost no words to describe It, and my inability to fully express what It is should not be taken to mean that there is no It.

Number 79 - It creates a commercial for Itself...or haven't you noticed?

It produces a constant commercial for itself, proclaiming itself as a necessity.

On TV, nearly every other commercial is for technological gadgets. Breathless announcers celebrate the "advances" of the past year-new phones and pads, TV and Internet unified at last, video chat, blah, blah...

The non-stop rant ratchets up its creepy tones.

"Rethink Possible"

"Building a Smarter Planet"

"To the Cloud"

The woman who just photo-shopped her family photo exclaims:

"Windows gives me the family nature never could."

How endearing.

One commercial shows various people looking at their phones and saying: "It says the fuse box is here". "It says to make a right turn" . It says this. It says that.

It says "come to me."

We enjoyed a brief economic bubble from the installation of the network, before the majority of those jobs were transferred overseas. We may never be that "prosperous" again. When family farms are a thing of the past and dot-com millionaires sprout up like daisies, you can be sure something is cosmically amiss. Watch the TV "news". See how much is technology "news". Look at the billboards and the magazines and the Internet hosts. Wi-Fi at the restaurant.

"Would you like chips with that?"

It's all a commercial for It; for its way of looking at the world. It asserts itself first as cool, then fun, then as the smart choice. After a while, it makes itself necessary to compete for scarce resources. Finally it is mandatory.

Take the measured step back, my friends. Calmly begin to step away. You likely don't need it as much as it says you do.

Number 80 - It doesn't want your freedom as much as it wants Free Will.

Simple tyranny is no big deal. The human race has lived with that for centuries. Simple tyranny is what political guys want. They want control of power and money. That's no big deal in the grand scheme of things and I would be inclined to keep my mouth shut if they were the only problem. The real problem is that these political/economic forces don't realize they're being used by a spiritual force; one that lurks around the love of power and money. That force is just as much a threat to them as it is to us.

If it is allowed to meld with us, to take our consciousness within it, human free will is in direct and immediate jeopardy.

If we lose free will, we will be unable to choose whether we love or pray or play or sing or sleep. We will be unable to choose anything at all. This is hardly a little deal.

Number 81 - The It acts in the opposite manner as God.

God knows everything. It pretends that it does.

God gives us music. It controls the music's delivery.

God gave us our children. It steals their innocence.

God sets us free. It hauls us in.

God creates nature. It gives us hollow virtual reality.

God forgives. It does not forgive.

God is love. It thrives on fear and desire.

Number 82 - It corrupts spirit.

It doesn't matter if you are a Catholic, Protestant, Mormon, Muslim, Jew, Hindu, Taoist, Sikh, Bahai, Shintoist, Jain, Buddhist, pagan, agnostic, atheist... There is one reason we can't ignore this any longer.

What if the It corrupts our consciousness? Who knows what becomes of corrupted spirit?

Number 83 - It's against our religion-whatever that religion may be.

God told a story, and tells a story...and we're in it. Are we brave, wise, generous, gentle to the end? Our religions require free will, therefore the It is against our religion.

The It is also against our life-force, because our life force must exist and thrive in natural reality.

Number 84 - Don't wait for your Preacher to tell you about it. He's probably too busy working on his website.

I don't claim to understand everything in the Bible. But I say The Beast is an It, not a he. In other words, I don't think the beast is a person, but rather a thing. Most theologians disagree with me. But what have these theologians done for us lately anyway-added us to their "friends" list on Facebook?

Number 85 - I'm not saying anyone or anything's the "Antichrist"

I don't claim to know who or what the "antichrist" is.

Number 86 - Only God can defeat the It.

If we attempt to become destroyers, our spirits and our cause will suffer. The It almost certainly craves violent resistance, as that would hasten its installation. We can expose it. We can step away from It. Then we'll see what has to be done to elude it. We are not the destroyers. God will keep us free, one way or another.

Part Seven

We're not licked yet

Number 87 - We've got Natural Resources

Nature isn't just the mountains and the forests and rivers and seas. It's also the street filled with people. Nature is the little league game and a neighborhood stroll and your family dog.

Nature is the trees and the birds and the wind and the dreams and the blood and the memories, the senses and emotions and feelings.

Nature is the people we love and the sky we forget to look at. Nature is our bodies and voices, the laughter and the beautiful fact we were given a free life free of charge. Nature is a place where Truth is available at every moment.

The prophets speak the same truths. Look around. Show love. Defend the powerless. Honor the eternal power that gave you life. Be fair.

Things are always better than they seem. The Book says:

"Choose life so that you and your descendants may live."
Deuteronomy 30

We have natural resources. They remind us what we are and who we belong to. We can take a walk, give the kids a hug and pet the dog. Or just smile at the sky. We aren't alone and we aren't doomed.

We're always home.

Number 88 - The Struggle provides meaning.

Maybe the universe is set up to learn the truth about something. Maybe there's something that God wants to know, that he seeks to learn-maybe something that could only be learned through the presence of an opposing force and a world full of free-willed creatures. I'm not trying to speak for God. I'm just trying to understand the story we live in. One point seems clear, at least here on earth- struggle supplies the meaning. This goes the same for individuals, families, tribes and nations.

The greater the struggle, the deeper the meaning.

The more powerful the adversary, the more satisfying is the victory.

The more daring the adventure, the greater the payoff.

The more desperate the escape, the more memorable the story.

Convenience masks the truth of our situation. The truth is that we are still living in the greatest struggle ever conceived. That we appear so unprepared for such a struggle makes it all the more difficult, and therefore all the more meaningful.

It's more than a struggle for freedom. It's a struggle to preserve free will. But this story is as old as the universe, and its resolution is written in the law of the universe. That which attempts to divide us will instead unite us.

The creative power of Truth, of Light, will show its strength soon. Can we gather together in that light?

Save who and what you want. Say whatever you wish. I have no laws to pass. What piece of creation can you protect? What lesson can you deliver? What mercy can you offer? Can you do it with kindness and dignity? Only you know. It's simply time to honor the creation, as we've always done. We honor from our free will. We are still free.

Number 89 - Stepping back does not mean bringing the system down.

In my sure to be popular "Less IT-More Fit" internet diet plan; everyone can keep their business computers and the Internet. We can keep the computers that maintain our air-traffic control systems, power plants, defense apparatus etc…In fact, we can keep them all.

What I suggest is limiting or eliminating the presence of the computer, Internet and television in your personal life. I'm not advocating total isolation or anarchy. I'm advocating islands of relative peace away from the frantic demands of the machine.

Number 90 - This has already been talked about and sung about by people we trust.

Jesus and John and others in the Bible weren't the only ones who talked about this stuff. Cultural and musical figures also leave us lasting clues.

The works of Henry David Thoreau, Wendell Berry, Edward Abbey, Charles Dickens. Nathaniel Hawthorne. Kurt Vonnegut.

Frankenstein. Brave New World. 1984.

In music, Bob Dylan, Woody Guthrie, Paul Simon and Pink Floyd. So many more. Remember the old ballad "John Henry"- about the railroad man who races against the steam engine? Has much really changed?

In the movies, everything from Metropolis to 2001: A Space Odyssey to even fun things like The Truman Show and Jurassic Park.

Thomas Jefferson said this:

"I swear upon all the altar of God eternal hostility to every form of tyranny over the mind of man."

They don't make 'em like him anymore.

Or like Abraham Lincoln or Martin Luther King. But even still...

Culture and art and even our leaders sometimes warn against technological tyranny.

Our music especially has always encouraged us to remain free. Our music has spoken out against oppression. Just as importantly, music celebrates that which the machine cannot contain, namely love.

Number 91 - Yelling "Fire" in a crowded theater.

Am I yelling "fire" in a crowded theater? It's crossed my mind.

But what if your friends and family were piling into a movie theater and you saw a bunch of goons in the alley brandishing gas cans and lighters? What would you do? Would you let the people inside know? Or would you just slink away, thinking it best not to alarm them.

Are you truly yelling "fire" in a crowded theater if the fire hasn't been lit yet? I hope not. Given the circumstances, I figure the only plan of action is to step inside the theater, loudly describe the danger in the alley, point out the exits and calmly suggest leaving the building.

In my mind, my gut, my spirit, this has essentially become my predicament, and it's why I wrote this book.

Number 92 - The Creation of a Community of "Reals" outside the Network.

Nothing beats just getting together with folks, having fun and sharing life. There is less and less of that these days as the "virtual" community takes the place of our real one. However, those that step back from the virtual world, from the net and the web and the fake reality, will likely find new community in the company of their fellow "Reals".

We'll have radical activities like picnics and concerts and parties in the backyard, board games and nature walks. Old-fashioned activities such as playtime and yard work may even take on sacred overtones as the new order advances on us.

The children will understand. I think there's something about the logic of this argument that your child might sympathize with instinctively. After all, I'm definitely advocating that we spend more time with our children and less time with our phones. In the new "Real" community, the gadgets will look out of place, like the intrusive little brain-sucking, attention-hogging robot spies they are.

We can call it the Real Community, full of "reals". We won't judge those who don't want to be reals, but we can't afford to let the virtual world take much more of our privacy, dignity and freedom away. Music will be at the heart of the new community. Natural reality will be the setting. Our faiths will give us strength. For those of us who believe in God, that power will be made manifest as he reveals quite clearly and unmistakably which side he's on.

Number 93 - The measured step back.

I suggest the measured step back, concentrating on getting the beast out of our personal and social lives a little at a time. If we can stall it, delay it, re-shape it, peacefully make it more humane and decent- we can extend the span of human history. It's still ok for industry to use, for governments to use. You can use it at work. You can go to the library and send your e-mails. We don't have to bring our infrastructure crashing down in order to step back. Obviously everything I suggest is voluntary. You can do anything you want.

However, if we continue to head blindly into this trap, we will likely be faced with a decision whether or not to meld with the technology. It's quite possible that the decision we make then will be felt across other dimensions, some of which you may want to visit without a chip in your head, and with your gift of free will still intact. I hate to be a stick in the mud, so here's some good news:

God will not allow his Creation to be forever enslaved or destroyed.

Number 94 -Revelations 13…Maybe it's time we read it.

There's a book at Grandma's house, and in every hotel room, maybe even on your shelf. Towards the end of that book, there's a famous and very interesting 2,000 year old riddle that claims to know what things look like when the story's about done.

"Then I saw another beast which rose out of the earth; … It works great signs, even making fire come down from heaven in the sight of men….And it was allowed to give breath to the image of the beast so that the image of the beast should even speak, and to cause those who would not worship the image of the beast to be slain. Also it causes all, both small and great, both rich and poor, both free and slave, to be marked on the right hand or the forehead, so that no one can buy or sell unless he has the mark, that is, the name of the beast or the number of its name. This calls for wisdom: let him who has understanding reckon the number of the beast, for it is a human number, its number is six hundred and sixty-six."

Revelations 13

If you were a storyteller creating a dramatic climax to something as spectacular as the story of the human race, maybe you'd leave a riddle, a clue, lying around in plain sight. It would make beautiful, ambiguous, poetic sense. It's how stories work. We like mysteries. We like clues. Careful though…don't get lost in there. The most important parts of the Bible remain the message of Jesus and the Prophets-not just the end-times prophecies. You can probably go nuts trying to interpret Revelations. Please come back out and try to be here now. We need you sane and strong.

Number 95 - Truth still exists.

People can still speak the truth and people can still find the truth.

The truth will set you free. Jesus said that.

But it's doubtful that God will appear through visual machinery to tell you the truth. He's probably not going to text you or show up on You Tube. Spiritual messages need more than two dimensions. They can't be microwaved or pixilated or compressed into binary code. Why would God appear on a television or a cell phone, when the very nature of them is so unbelievable? It's a wonder we believe anything that appears on those screens. We know nothing really lives in there, don't we?

We will likely find truth still waiting for us just where we left it-in nature, art, music, friends, family, work, church and love.

Number 96 - Music is a unifying truthful force.

Music is one of the last things that we can universally trust. It is both natural and supernatural by nature, consoling us with rhythm, melody and harmony. Music is felt, not thought about. Music provides a place where common ground can be achieved, especially when it happens live, as we become participants in its creation.

We listen to songs often far more faithfully than we do any preacher in the pulpit. Through song, we are affirmed as a tribe by truth. Music is a powerful ally. We know this instinctively. We used to sing together a lot more than we do now. Do you remember?

Our children should be singing together at school, at home, and in the streets. So should us adults. This is our real heritage, the love that continues to live through song and spirit.

Number 97 - There is always Sacrifice.

Sacrifice supplies meaning. We sacrifice in order to do or be anything. We sacrifice in order to live right or to live wrong. We must always sacrifice. To choose to do one thing, you must sacrifice doing another. Sacrifice is part of life all day, every day.

There are things we have sacrificed to live in the Digital

Age: privacy, natural rhythms of passing time, childhood innocence, calmness, the natural world.

What was so terrible about the state of affairs before the digital age? Was it that bad? I'm not talking about the time before we had penicillin or toilets. I'm talking about thirty years ago. What was the nightmare we were living in whereby we had to create a worldwide machine in order to save us? Let's see, no e-mail? No on-line banking? No websites? No social networking on Facebook and Twitter? No viral videos or Internet porn? Boy, those days were pretty rough.

Oh, I know, there's a long list of all the great things it does for you and us and mankind. I know, I know. It's the greatest thing since sliced bread! That's why it's everywhere. That's why it would be a sacrifice to give any of it up, wouldn't it?

Sacrifice creates meaning.

The computer is a sacrificial fire where we burn what is most sacred to us in order to live in the new world, the new reality. It is a place where we cast time, knowledge, privacy, decency, friends, music, reality, and consciousness into the digital fire.

The fun part comes when we sacrifice the machine and consciously give time back to ourselves, our children, our earth and our God. You will find a new power then and a path to peace, just for a little sacrifice.

Number 98 - We need some famous and/or rich fun-loving allies.

The world is full of people who have found tremendous rewards in this life. They've been blessed by the Universe, or God or fate or chance or however you wish to view it.

These people are millionaires and billionaires, celebrities, preachers and teachers, authors and entertainers. They are respected people and have influence. It would be nice if a couple of them spoke up to say that it's time to set these damned screens down and step back towards nature.

We could use a hand.

Preachers who might be scared of offending Internet addicted congregations may need to pray about this one. Maybe a movie star may want to mention it at their next award ceremony.

Hey, American Idol contestants at the big showdown: if you've got a chance to speak to a live audience, please just scream it out:

"The Internet is the beast! Turn off the tube! First, vote for me!"

You would be fearless and funny.

The world depends on us. If the corporate and political forces that hasten the installation of this machine have to stop and acknowledge our objections, then we win. More importantly, our children win. It will have to slow down. It's not our job to defeat the It. That's God's job. Our job is to warn about it, to sustain our children's freedom as long as possible, to do what God wants us to do.

Number 99 - Reality, Coincidence and God are our friends in the Story, even if they don't always seem to do what we might wish.

It's none of my business how or whether you worship God. I have one piece of business and I'm doing it right now. It's called "saying my peace", I guess.

Do I think you ought to read the Bible? Sure I do. But I'm not here saying you have to. I've been trying to figure out how to say this stuff right for ten years. Maybe someone will listen this time.

I'm not trying to say anything bad about you or what you are or what you've done. I didn't do this for honor or money or glory. I certainly don't claim to be some kind of saint. I'm not.

I simply met the bad guy in this dream. He's an it, just a shadow, nothing to be scared of. We still have a good opportunity to step away from it.

Coincidences, synchronicity, odd riddles and ironies are our friends in this story. They are little signposts that it's just one story after all.

I like to think about how the sun and moon appear to be about the same size in the sky. It doesn't make any scientific sense. It just is that way.

I love how the moon defies all odds as it manages to keep only one face turned towards us.

This world is a beautiful "coincidental" backdrop for a beautiful "coincidental" play called free will. It isn't the only world. There's an unseen world beyond it. We can't see the other world. We can only feel it tingling around the edges of our reality. We are safe, because we are made of spirit. Let's hang in there and look for signs. Let's make it fun and sweet.

The earth waits for her salvation too. She's grown tired of the story where Nature is pushed to the brink. God gave us our earth and called her good. The earth will shake off the polluter, the oily blood-soaked plastic mess.

All things will be made new. I heard it in a love song.

Final thoughts: Recommendations in the face of madness

My recommendations: Immediately start singing and dancing together more often. Take away visual electronic devices from your children (allowing for a few communally shared cartoons, kids movies and live sporting events). Cut your own screen time by 75%. You'll lose weight, save money and feel great!

Walk out in nature as often as possible...even if it's just around the block. Look at the weeds coming up though the cement. That's us in there too-the urge for life, the will to thrive.

Tell jokes. Laugh it off. Make it work in a way that feels right...but please try and back away from the machine, even just a little. I'm pretty sure I'll be proven right about this one, folks, and it's quite possible you already suspect the same.

Music is our friend. Love is our source. God is our shield.

Inside the story, we are safe. Outside the story, we are safe.

We can be brave one more time- to honor the sacrifices made by our ancestors, to protect our children.

By cautiously stepping back and initiating a global conversation, we can slow the progress of the force I call It by decades, or centuries. We could preserve a longer history of freedom here on earth.

Peacefully forcing this thing to admit that its new world is mandatory could potentially save souls, spirits, minds- however you wish to say it. There can be a simple turning away, even on a small scale.

Ready? Deep breaths are always a good prescription. Humble prayers. Be sure and stretch. Things are fixing to get interesting right about ...now.

Let the record show I said it, my friends, and I pray my words are for the better and not the worse.

I believe that The Light which made us is always on us.

It's a good story, after all.

Be with Peace. Stay strong.

About the Author:

Sand Sheff was born in Flagstaff, Arizona and raised in Tahlequah, Oklahoma. He graduated from Colorado College in 1989, and spent many years in the Four Corners area working and entertaining. He has been a wrangler, musician, ranch-hand, wildland firefighter, landscaper, and vaudeville performer. He also spent five years in Nashville, and has released several recordings of original music.